THE INVISIBLE WALLS OF DANNEMORA

INSIDE THE INFAMOUS CLINTON CORRECTIONAL FACILITY

STATE OF NEW YORK - DEPARTMENT OF CORRECTIONAL SERVICES

CLINTON CORRECTIONAL FACILITY

Date:________________, 20____

From: ***M. Blaine,*** Lieutenant

To: ____

Subject: ____

____ Return with more details - **Incomplete**

____ Please answer [send me a copy]

____ See me about this

____ Prepare draft for my signature by ______________________

____ ***Central Office Inquiry - Priority Response***______________

____ Take appropriate action

____ Note and Return with your comments by__________________

____ ***Superintendent's Inquiry - Priority Response By***__________

____ For your information

____ Investigate and report by __________________________

COMMENTS: ______________________________________

____

____

____

____

____

____

____

____

Adm./241

MICHAEL H. BLAINE

THE INVISIBLE WALLS OF DANNEMORA

INSIDE THE INFAMOUS CLINTON CORRECTIONAL FACILITY

GAUDIUM

Gaudium Publishing
Las Vegas ◊ Oxford ◊ Palm Beach

Published in the United States of America by
Histria Books, a division of Histria LLC
7181 N. Hualapai Way
Las Vegas, NV 89166 USA
HistriaBooks.com

Library of Congress Control Number: 2020932528

ISBN 978-1-59211-043-8 (hardcover)
ISBN 978-1-59211-046-9 (softbound)

Table of Contents

THE INVISIBLE WALLS OF DANNEMORA

INSIDE THE INFAMOUS CLINTON CORRECTIONAL FACILITY

BADGE# 17069
BLAINE. MICHAEL
CORRECTION OFFICER
9/27/88

Preface

Nothing escapes the effects of time. Oscar Wilde wrote: "With age comes wisdom, but sometimes age comes alone." Such was the case at the now-famous Clinton Correctional Facility, simply referred to by most as "Clinton" or "Dannemora." I will utilize these names as well throughout my story. Despite its formidable appearance, the aging maximum-security facility in Dannemora, New York, morphed and mutated over time, along with its employees and inmates. Unfortunately, wisdom became a commodity throughout the years. Leadership transferred or retired, and obedient Central Office (or better known as Building 2) soldiers in cheap suits with their marching orders took over the administrative reins. Sycophants amongst the staff - especially in the union leadership - made themselves known and wormed their way into their new master's favor. The facility was simply never the same afterward. It slowly deteriorated and it became more apparent with each promotion that I took. I would return to this facility by which I judged all others.

The many changes within Clinton, as well as its administrations and staff over the years, contributed to the first successful escape by two convicted murderers, inmates Matt and Sweat. These changes were never cited in the laughable "official" escape report, which should have been titled, "As told by inmate Sweat." Regardless, these changes took place and nothing was done to correct them. This is my first-hand account.

Though this book incorporates much of my personal life in that horrific place, it is important to understand how my service changed me and those around me - some for the better, some not. As a good friend and former co-worker said just before the completion of this book, "The staff was a compilation of everything, from Nikola Tesla to Forrest Gump." No truer words have ever been spoken.

The public cannot even begin to fathom the daily challenges that we faced, the injustices suffered, as well as the personal agendas and vendettas that I witnessed and endured. Camaraderie and laughter at times solidified us and some lifelong friendships developed; other staff we hoped to never see again. Few people realized that we were all a product of our environment and were consumed by it. What could some of my co-workers have possibly experienced to make them the way they were?

When Clinton experienced the first successful escape in its incredible history, everyone suddenly became an expert on the subject. Stolen valor by some claiming to have played a role at Clinton was rampant. Not a single person who wrote a book on the subject had worked 9,523 days, or 26 years and 27 days, like myself. Some were simply trainees for a few weeks over twenty-five years earlier. None had seen or experienced the things that those of us who called Clinton home had. It was a well-known fact that if you could work at Clinton, you could work anywhere. If you had been on the Clinton day tour count desk, upper F Block 1st Officer, or unlucky enough to be thrown into the main chart sergeant jobs, you knew that you could go to any other facility and shine. Those are some of the most thankless jobs that New York State has to offer and yet the staff did them without complaint. Everyone at Clinton has stories to share. You simply cannot be exposed to such an environment and expect to leave it behind when you leave. A part of you simply stays behind, unable to walk out the front gate for the last time.

Although all the events and experiences described in this book occurred as described, the names of the individuals mentioned in the story have been changed, except for those on public record.

Meeting Gene

The sun was high in the sky on that hot, sunny day in the summer of '86. Fresh off our Peru, NY farm at 19, I was tall, lean, and strong from years of hard farm living. I sat down on some stacked lumber and opened my cooler to eat my lunch. The boss and most of the crew had already headed to a local diner. Despite the smell and the noise from the farm equipment and animals, I quietly reflected on the first half of the day. It seemed to have gone pretty smoothly on my first day as a laborer for a contractor that primarily built barns in the northern New York region.

I wasn't alone. About 10 feet away was a tall, thin, 28-year-old fellow laborer with sunburned, white, freckled skin, and long, flaming red hair down to his shoulders. We hadn't spoken during the day, as we worked in different spots of the site. He broke the silence with his surprisingly soft and gentle voice. "So, what do you think?" he asked with a smile. Small talk ensued and the friendship quickly solidified. I soon learned that he was a guitar player in a small rock band in the area. Both of us had taken different civil service exams for New York State Correction Officer and we both had equal hopes of securing jobs in the prison system. Little did I realize that I had just met future Correction Officer Gene Palmer, the man who would unknowingly contribute to the first successful escape from the Clinton Correctional Facility on June 6, 2015.

Within a few months, I tired of the hard work at a low wage. Being pressured to work most weekends and having to ask for my overtime pay just was not, in any way, appealing to me. Whenever work was rained out I took advantage of the downtime as I looked for better jobs and filled out applications. One particularly desirable job was at a local wallpaper mill. The head of the personnel department was a kind, older gentleman who sent me for a physical and told me that he would be calling. Trying to do the right thing and not leave the contractor blindsided and shorthanded, I informed the boss that I would probably be getting the call soon. He and his son were relentless in their snide comments. A few weeks later, I received the call to report to the mill that afternoon. As I picked up my tools, Gene wanted to know how the boss had handled my leaving. I filled him in on how nasty he and his son had become towards me. "Fuck 'em," he said with a playful smile. Fuck 'em indeed. I was walking away and I had no intention of ever returning. I never looked back, not even once.

The Road To Harriman

Away I went and started at the mill that afternoon. The work was routine and tedious. The pay was great, but it was clearly a dead end. Some of the guys were wonderful to work with, but I was mostly surrounded by drunks and locals with little ambition. I had dreams of achieving more. They were happy in their routine. I patiently waited. I simply could not do over 40 years in this place. I wanted more. I had to get out.

It was while I was working at the mill that I met my future wife, Helen. I had stopped at the local mall after trying to get my hockey skates sharpened. She was flirtatious and we made small talk. She had a part-time job at the local movie theater, as well as being a secretary in Clinton's mental health unit. We enjoyed each other's company and the relationship developed. Her family was strange, to say the least, but they were seemingly tolerable.

Then one day I received a notice in the mail from New York State asking if I was still interested in employment as a Correction Officer – or C.O. I filled out the form indicating my interest and mailed it back that same day. Helen was livid that I did so. "Those guys are such assholes," she whined when I told her about the notice, but this was my future, not hers.

Within a few months, I received another notice from the New York State Department of Civil Service. I opened my mail and read the letter. "Do not report for your physical unless you are at least 20 years and 9 months of age," the notice stated. Panic set in. 1, 2, 3, 4, 5, 6 ,7 ,8, 9! I counted out loud and with excitement. I would be 20 years, 9 months and 9 days on the date of the physical!

I had never been as far as Albany before this trip. Although it was only 150 miles from my home, I stayed at a hotel the night before so I would be on time the next day. Nervous and feeling out of place, the next morning I reported to my physical. I was young, in great shape, and I could not believe how easy it was. The nurses who conducted the testing kept commenting on my age and I would simply smile and nod. A month or so later, I reported for the psychological portion of the exam. I sat in front of the psychologist who reviewed my file and broke the silence by asking me, "Why do you hate your mother?" I was shocked and speechless but I finally managed to say that I did not hate my mother. He insisted, "Of course you do." Again I said no. He said, "I have to put something down here... give me something...." I thought and thought... "S-s-s-she burns her cookies!" I blurted. He started laughing out loud. "You're fine. We'll see you soon," he said, continuing to laugh as I exited the office. Now I had to await the next notice in the mail.

The letter finally came. I was to report to the Harriman Training Academy on the evening of Sunday, June 26, 1988, for training. I made the preparations and gathered the items listed in the notice. Laundry bag, t-shirts, underwear, socks, uniform shoes, workout gear. Everything was in order. I had given ample notice to the mill and thanked them repeatedly for the job. I was more than happy to get away from that crew of misfits. I felt free as I walked out for the last time and never looked back. Helen and I had been on the outs, but we still communicated.

My suitcase was packed and I was ready to roll as I awaited my ride that Sunday afternoon. A friend of mine, Aaron, had started weeks earlier and I gladly accepted his offer to carpool with him and his classmate, Ronald. We chatted freely as we made the nearly five-hour journey down the interstate. We grabbed a little dinner just before reaching the academy. Dressed in my dark suit and tie, they explained the ins and outs of academy life and what to expect. I was all ears.

We approached the academy. It was rumored that the facility had been a convent at one time. It was a nice, peaceful setting, except for the wildfires burning in the region which left a film on everything and caused me non-stop sinus issues. Deer could be seen grazing on its well-manicured lawns in the mornings. Hoofprints were everywhere, which excited us rural recruits who enjoyed venison. I waited in line with several other recruits for admission and processing. We kept moving up in line and I was now the first person in line. It was now my turn to be greeted.

Officer Ricardo greeted me at the front door. He was a short, incredibly fit, late middle-aged Hispanic man with an impeccable Class A uniform and shiny uniform shoes. After looking me up and down, he challenged me, asking if I could make my shoes shine like his. "Yes, sir," I replied since we were both were wearing patent leather uniform shoes that always shined. With a wipe of a rag and a little furniture polish, they were mirrors. He then directed me inward.

Inside the academy were the processing stations. Information was taken and cross-checked, sizes taken, gray, "Class B" uniforms issued, bedding and room assignments given. Nobody said a word about the fact that I was not yet 21 years of age. They weren't asking and I wasn't telling. I just did as I was told and moved along with the others. I met my roommate, a local from my county, thoroughly cleaned my half of the room, made my bed, and cleaned up. I then fell asleep in nervous anticipation of the next day.

Harriman

The morning of Monday, June 27, 1988, was here. This date would become as important to me as a Social Security number. I was now a member of Correction Officer Recruit Training Class 88-7A. In between filling out seemingly endless forms and several different speakers, we were addressed by Lieutenant Corey. He was a big, gruff man with white hair, and bore an incredible resemblance to Archie Bunker in the TV comedy, *All In The Family*. "If you look good, you will feel good," he thundered as he spoke from the podium and looked down upon us. For the next six weeks, we would learn physical training, marching, contraband, transporting of inmates, directives, report writing, legals, weapons, chemical agents, unarmed defensive tactics, restraints, and all other aspects of the correctional services. I was attentive and applied myself. As long as you gave 100%, the instructors left you alone. One fact they revealed before investing too much time into us was that 85% of us would end up divorced. A collective gasp of shock and disbelief was heard. There's no way that could be accurate. So many, just like myself, felt that their relationships or marriages could withstand anything. How naive we were.

The academy life was pretty simple with its routine. Each morning, except Mondays, started with physical training first thing in the morning, followed by a run. Then came showers and breakfast, before marching off to classes as a unit. More marching and calling cadence, lunch, classes, and more marching to dinner. Our downtime was filled with foosball, studying, and preparing for the next day.

I turned 21 during the third week of training, which dealt with weapons. It was nice to be away from the classrooms for the week. My friends took me out to celebrate. Being an inexperienced drinker, I soon felt no pain. The very next day I had to qualify with the department rifle – the AR-15. I qualified with the weapon despite my hangover. BOOM! BOOM! BOOM! echoed through my head with each squeeze of the trigger, despite my protective headphones. The rifle's assault on my senses made shooting it quite a bit tougher. The little .223 caliber round was as impressive as it was effective. The departmental sidearm was a .38 Special Model 10 Smith and Wesson revolver. Having never used a handgun previously, I thoroughly enjoyed the weapon and easily achieved upper-level scores. All was well as we safely enjoyed the range, then moved on to the departmental Remington 870P 12-gauge shotgun. It was during this portion of range week that I started to observe behaviors that caused me to take notice. I began to see a pattern of unequal application of rules and discipline. I could not possibly imagine how much worse it would become throughout the years.

During one part of the shotgun training, we were to demonstrate a riot control technique in front of an instructor. One by one we would take control of the weapon, just like we had been trained, make it safe and clear, load it, and wait to be called up to the firing line. We watched as a thin, female recruit was literally lifted off the ground – either by recoil, reaction, or a combination thereof, and threw the shotgun onto the ground. A cease-fire was called and she began to scream at the instructor, "I am not shooting it again! I don't have to. I'm not going to and you can't make me, either!" She simply refused to budge on the issue. Several of us looked at each other in disbelief. "Talk to an instructor like that?" "How can she get away with that?" "They'll boot her ass out for that!" my fellow recruits whispered to one another. An instructor pulled her aside and talked to her as we finished qualifying for that portion of the day. She remained behind as we returned to the academy. Later, we learned that she miraculously qualified with that same weapon after we had left. Funny how that happens.

Certain portions of the training remained with you throughout the years. One that stuck to me like glue regarded manipulation of staff and informants. The instructors drilled into us that manipulation starts with something small. It could be as simple as an inmate asking for something small, trying to engage in small talk, then it progresses and develops without the staff member realizing it. With female staff, it could be something as seemingly innocent as a comment about their appearance or inquiring about their weekend. All staff had to be vigilant about these things, as they could develop into full-fledged relationships. Prison informants only provide information when it benefits them. This could be purposefully misleading information to draw your attention away from their own unauthorized activities or to gain special favors such as staff looking the other way for committing minor infractions, or to seek leniency from hearing officers during disciplinary hearings for more serious offenses. Somebody always wanted something. Everything happens for a reason.

During my fifth week, we received our blue Class A uniforms as the end of training rapidly approached. One evening, at a bar, an instructor loosened up and disclosed to me that the academy sergeant, a short, balding, little man with a big attitude, had noticed my age during the initial processing. This was a big deal since you had to be 21 years of age to become a peace or police officer in New York State. He had made some phone calls but was told by Central Office to let me stay. I would be 21 before graduation. That same sergeant many years later was a Deputy Superintendent at a maximum security facility. It was rumored that he had a drinking issue. One night he pulled into his facility for a midnight round and, unknowingly, nearly caught two convicts escaping. The cons later disclosed that they thought they had been seen, and were about to give themselves up. They then realized that the guy never saw them and away they went. One of the inmates, Vaile, and I would cross paths later in my career.

Week six was here and we were crisp and sharp. Reality began to sink in when we were herded into the auditorium for a serious topic: Hostage Training. That very week, hostages had been taken at the Coxsackie Correctional Facility and it made for seemingly endless, intense discussion. You could hear a pin drop as we took our seats. The TV and VCR were on a cart before us and the discussion began. The instructors told us sternly that we were to watch a video of the Sing Sing hostage-taking of 1983. Toward the end, as it showed the hostages being released, staff abruptly stopped the video because a staff member, who had been a hostage, preferred that their image not be shown. They urged us to be sensitive to their wishes should we deduce who it was. It didn't take us long to pinpoint the person. Later in my career, I would have the honor of working with a few of his fellow hostages. They were stand up guys who found themselves nearly in the middle of the Clinton riot later that same year. In this incident, the inmates refused to leave the north yard. The inmates had believed false information about an inmate involved in a use of force incident and it had prompted the demonstration. Once the sergeant had gotten his staff out of the yard and the officer in 12 Post fired 22 rounds into second base on the ball field, it helped convince the inmates to exit the yard and return to their cells. They had no bargaining power. Their cause was lost.

The training for class 88-7A was now complete. Helen had driven down with Fred's girlfriend the night before for our graduation party. Everyone had an incredible time and cut loose. The next day, as we awaited graduation, I saw them walk up outside. It was the first time I had seen Helen wear a dress. I was shocked. It had become an issue between us. We proudly received our diplomas and badges as we graduated on that Friday morning with the typical New York State pomp and circumstance baloney that I would come to loathe. I was headed to the

The author marching with his graduating class (front right)

Clinton Correctional Facility with a good-sized group of our class for on the job training, otherwise referred to as OJT. Our OJT assignments were based on our region. They assigned you to be trained for four weeks at the maximum-security facility nearest to your home. I had the weekend off with Helen, but I anxiously awaited Monday at Clinton.

Clinton

I drove up Route 374 to Dannemora with anticipation. As I maneuvered the final bend, the immense, sprawling grounds of Clinton Correctional Facility appeared. It seemed to go on forever and it became more ominous as I approached the massive wall with strategically placed armed wall posts. I had not traveled up there very often in the past. Upon arriving, we were directed to the training cottage - an old, gray, stone structure with rooms for classroom training. Every sound echoed throughout the old building. On the walls were a few historic photos depicting Clinton's proud past, which oozed with history and dated back to 1845. This made Clinton the third oldest facility and the state's largest with nearly 3,000 inmates.

I had some history here as well. My Uncle Clifford had been a prison guard here from the late 40s to the mid-50s. He was a WWI veteran and had preferred the calm and quiet of an assignment on tuberculosis or TB Hill. It was just outside of the prison wall and up on the hill behind the prison where the state-owned houses now sit. My cousin Nathan worked there as an officer from 1974-1986 when he chose to transfer to a smaller facility.

After being herded into a classroom, our day consisted of being greeted by the training staff and addressed by the Training Lieutenant, filling out forms, having our photos taken, orientation and tour of both the Maximum A facility, referred to as the "Main," and the Maximum B facility referred to as the "Annex." It was all a blur. No matter where we went, staff closely looked at our name tags to see if we were related to

Lineup and roll call for Clinton staff in the 1950s

anyone worth acknowledging. First, we toured the Main, which was surrounded by its wall, shielding from view this condensed city of cell blocks, mess halls with scenic murals painted on its walls, industry, as well as the special housing unit, or more commonly referred as the SHU. Clinton's SHU had a unique designation: Unit 14 or "The Unit". The tour continued through the very unique North Yard complete with a ski jump, ball field and little fenced-off properties in the side of the hill called "courts." These courts, complete with crude furniture, firewood and a cookstove made from old 55-gallon drums, allowed inmates not under disciplinary sanctions to hang out and cook meals. The Annex portion of Clinton was much less intriguing, with its dormitories and fences topped with concertina wire. This facility had previously been the Dannemora State Hospital for the Criminally Insane from 1900-1975, complete with its own, long-forgotten bowling alley in the basement that required the pins to be set by hand. Upon ending its mission as a state hospital, it then took on a role similar to its function today. My Uncle Henry had worked there for years and through all of the transitions, retiring in 1978.

No matter where our tour through the facility took us, you were bombarded with the sights, sounds and smells of institutional life; the echoing through the halls, the unexciting shades of green and brown paint on the walls, the stench of humans unwilling or unable to practice proper hygiene living together. I recall immediately comparing it to our farm and how much nastier this place was. No matter where I worked, or what promotion I would take, it would be consistent throughout my career. No matter where I went, things were pretty much the same everywhere. At Clinton, it was just a harder-core version of it.

The first day was over and we were dismissed. My real education would start when I returned on Wednesday. I had been given Tuesday as a day off since I was to work the upcoming weekend.

The Real Training Begins

I was excited to begin my career, although I had no idea what lay before me. The assignment or "chart" sergeant, Sgt. Swanson, paired me up with Stoney Roberts, the 1st Officer of Upper F Block. I quickly learned that Stoney, a martial artist, was one of the toughest men to have ever worked at Clinton. He was a tall, thin, genuinely nice guy who had nothing to prove to anyone. He showed much patience and taught me a great deal on that first day. When I followed Stoney's instructions not to open the utility, or "slop" sink, for anyone on the upper deck row of cells, known as a "company," I followed it to the letter. An inmate repeatedly asked me to open it up and I refused. The inmate hung his head, refusing to make eye contact as he said, "Officer, I know Mr. Roberts told you to not open the slop sink for anyone, but I need to get in there. You see, it is part of my job." He continued, "You are doing the right thing and I'm telling you, nobody will ever go against that man. Nobody!" I began to chuckle to myself and I admired the respect Stoney had earned. I opened the sink for him and he dove into his work. Later that day, I spoke with Stoney and he laughed as I told him about the encounter. He waved his hand like a king overlooking his realm and said, "He didn't lie. No inmate here will go against me!" Later in the afternoon, he sent me with his block porters, inmate workers assigned to various tasks and jobs, to the facility laundry. The porters headed out of the block and I called them to stop. I sheepishly asked Stoney where it was located. He laughed and began to give me directions in this massive place. He saw that I was confused and pointed to one of the porters and said, "Get him there and get him back!" Away we went and I somehow returned to the block with the same number of cons in short order. Once again, the respect for this man was clear.

I never forgot Stoney when he left the department and I saw him only occasionally throughout the years. A few years after my retirement, I ran into him on a sidewalk in Plattsburgh. He had a confused look on his face as I approached, and I called out to him, "Don't you recognize your old trainees?" He began to chuckle as I introduced myself and thanked him as I shook his hand. I shared these same stories with him and we both began to laugh. Behind his long beard, he smiled and seemed shocked that someone would take the time to let him know what an impression he had made upon them. It did a lot of good for us both.

On my second day, I was assigned to the Special Housing Unit – Unit 14. This disciplinary unit was reserved for inmates who committed the worst of offenses within the prison, such as assault on staff, escape, riot, weapons, or who were simply held there under an administrative segregation designation. Administrative segregation was utilized to isolate inmates deemed too dangerous for the general population. The system could keep an inmate isolated for years with internal appeals to fight for their release back into the population. Some cons preferred the safety and isolation of the Unit rather than risking their reputation and asking for Protective Custody or P.C. Fairly often, inmates would commit one of the most serious of prison offenses just to get assigned to the SHU.

The day shift was a hubbub of activity. Chow, yard, showers, laundry, medical callouts, and whatever might pop up during the tour of duty. Sgt. Swanson was our supervisor for the day. He had a cheerful, magnetic personality and knew how to get things done. Little did I know that I would only meet his equal one other time in my career. The inmates had sufficient time to eat their breakfast. Some were fed a diet of cabbage and nutri-loaf. This was referred to as a "Restricted Diet" and was a last resort in discipline. It was nasty, but it met all of the nutritional requirements. After the collection of garbage, we then began to take them out to the yards, one by one, for their hour of recreation. Trainees like me would typically be brought to the lockbox area for that particular row of cells and shown how to operate the controls. After that, we were given a set of keys and the recreation/shower list and waited for the signal to open or close the cells. The employee graffiti in the lockbox areas provided me with a fair amount of amusement. The one saying that I still use to this day is, "Be Alert. The world needs more Lerts!"

I was assigned to the unit a few times during my training at Clinton. On the second occasion, I was watching the yard through a window and noticed two inmates in boxing stances, squared off, and the fists began to fly. I hurried to the yard door with the other officers. Sgt. Swanson was his usual calm, cool, collected and cheerful self. He blocked the door and, with a smile, told us to wait as we watched the fight outside. The fight was a pretty fair matchup, but nothing lasts forever. We soon had a winner and a loser. The fight had been decided. One inmate was now sitting on the chest of the other and pounding away with his fists. Sgt. Swanson, with all of us around him, walked up to the victor, placed a hand on his shoulder and softly said, "It's over." Like God himself had ordered him to stop, the inmate complied, stood up and placed his hands behind his back, and walked to his cell. No use of force, no assault on staff, no insults. No hard feelings. Just two inmates who had an issue that had to be resolved. I was in awe.

A few hours later, we got the call. The captain would be coming up to do Tier III disciplinary hearings on some of the Coxsackie riot participants. A few had been transferred to Clinton's SHU to face their discipline. Everyone got to work as the kitchen/breakroom was transformed into a hearing office in minutes. The captain set up his paperwork and tape recorder and told the sergeant that he was ready for the inmate. The inmate emerged from his cell in restraints and we escorted him to his hearing. After the hearing was completed and the inmate learned of his disciplinary sanctions, we escorted him back to his barren cell. He had looked pretty rough and ragged as he hobbled into the hearing, restrained, but now he looked even worse. The captain had imposed years of Special Housing Unit sanctions upon him. Justice had been served as well as it could be within the department. He would still face criminal charges.

The last time that I was assigned to the unit was on a beautiful, warm weekend. Shortly after the noon meal was served to the inmates in their cells and the trash collected, we sat in the officers' kitchen/break room area. It wasn't long before Sgt. Swanson appeared with a pan of mess hall roast beef and a few loaves of bread from the noon meal. He set it before us and said, "Eat!" All of the trainees looked at each other, knowing that the fine for eating state food was $2,500. We all were thinking the same thing: We were being set up and tested. Nobody moved.

The sergeant clearly saw our apprehension. "I said eat!" he barked at us as he pointed at the food on the table. We scrambled to obey as we slapped the shoe leather-tough roast beef between slices of bread and wolfed it down. A half-hour later, he reappeared and kicked us out of the break room. "We've got business to do in here," he said as he pointed toward the door, and out we went. We all moved to the adjoining office and kicked back and relaxed in the chairs with full stomachs. The fan hummed and unknowingly lulled us to sleep. Sometime later, I opened my eyes. I had fallen asleep… we all had fallen asleep! My buddies were still fast asleep in their chairs and I heard laughter coming from the break room. Incredibly thirsty, I knocked on the door to get a drink and was told to come in. As the door opened, I witnessed the business they were attending to… a card game!

Clinton's mess hall was just like many others, but bigger. There was an East and West Mess, with the kitchen in between. Rows and rows of stainless steel table tops with swing-out metal seats. It was a sign of respect for one inmate to sit and swing-out the next seat for the next inmate. Over the years and on more than one occasion, I witnessed an inmate approach his seat only to discover that a less than observant inmate had failed to swing-out. The offended inmate typically would stand there for a moment, shaking his head, and then seat himself. Sometimes, they would gently remind their neighbor of the lack of respect shown, with the offender snapping to as they realized their error and apologetically swinging out the seat. Other times, the disrespect was intentional due to an inmate's body odor, mental state, or sexual preference. They simply were not wanted.

A variety of pictures painted by inmates over the years added some scenery to the otherwise cold, harsh room. I accompanied an officer as he escorted his company of inmates to the West Mess. Each mess hall could hold hundreds of inmates. As we approached the mess, the sergeant directed the inmates to which serving line they were to go. As we passed the sergeant, we gave him the block and company information, as well as the number of inmates we were escorting. We took our position watching the serving line, making sure that each and every inmate picked up their utensils - even if they were not eating. This was necessary since each inmate was responsible for displaying them to the officer and then depositing them in a collection bin as they exited the mess. After rotating from watching the serving line to supervising the seating, the sergeant gave us the nod to leave. Without a single word, the officer simply pointed toward the door and our group rose from their seats, utensils in hand, and headed out. I asked my trainer, "How do you know if we have the right guys?" He smiled and told me, "There is one of me and 40 of them. They know who they came with. It's their responsibility to leave with the right group."

The rest of my training at Clinton paled in comparison. Assignments to cell blocks, the mess hall, and other tedious tasks just weren't as appealing. Everyone has a job preference. Some guys preferred to bounce around as an escort, others were fine with supervising inmates in the shops, still others liked the solitude of wall posts. It took a special kind of officer to work the cell blocks. It was a job that I never learned to like.

Blocks are typically three levels high with rows of cells, called a company, on either side, facing outwards. Clinton's blocks were far from typical. Since the facility was built on the side of a mountain, some blocks had more tiers on one side than others, and some blocks were incredibly high and split into two blocks. In the winter, the top tiers would be roasting in heat and the lowest level freezing their asses off. In the summer, the blocks were stifling. I swear that in the humid summer months you could practically hear the place sweating. Roaches were everywhere and a smart employee would shake out their jacket, search their lunch box and never take their shoes into their house.

Being an effective block officer means that you will take on the roles of landlord, mayor, traffic cop, postman, garbage man, employer, counselor, inspector, secretary, and clerk. Trying to maintain a secure block with the nonstop movement of mess hall and program runs, cell moves, clean up, laundry and garbage runs, while somehow doing rounds of the block and attending to any emergency, kept you on the move. The public misconception of lazy, fat jail guards sitting around simply could not be any further from the truth. Some officers simply were good at this job and knew their block and inmates incredibly well. They often received valuable intelligence from informants which resulted in weapons being recovered or other events prevented from happening.

I never liked being confined to a block, especially as a two-week vacation fill-in or due to someone taking a sick or personal day. You were always working in someone else's house. The inmates were used to them, they had their own system and you were locked into a box. There is no space, no space to get away and collect your thoughts. When guys were going through a divorce, I would discreetly seek them out to talk with them in private, understanding from my own experience that working in a jail, unable to simply leave, only added to the stress level. I gave countless referrals to the Employee Assistance Program coordinator. This was a simple, confidential heads-up that an employee was facing an issue and may need a confidential ear or other available services. The employee in charge of this program while I was a supervisor did a great job assisting staff. I greatly appreciated him because I was offered no such assistance from the previous program coordinator when I'd needed help.

The second half of the facility training was in the Annex. The dormitories and more senior staff on the night shift made for very long and quiet evenings. On the weekend I was assigned to the Recreation Officer. We froze our asses off in the yard as the wind blew on that August day. We tried to keep warm as we wrapped ourselves in bright orange NYSDOCS raincoats. Only a single tower or "guard post" overlooked us. The old, weathered, rickety tower looked like it would fall over with a strong wind. The officer inside was a slight but cheerful guy who joked back and forth with the officers on the ground. That same officer, many years later, would become a sergeant and ended up retiring after a serious on-duty assault by an inmate. A few years later, he briefly eluded the authorities after killing his ex-girlfriend and her boyfriend. He was convicted of first-degree murder and he will die in prison.

Our on-the-job training was rapidly winding down. We received our facility assignments and prepared ourselves for the unknown length of time that we would be away. Along with some of my closer academy friends, I was assigned to the Fishkill Correctional Facility. It was a medium-security facility and it sure beat the hell out of being assigned to Sing Sing or Bedford Hills. I counted my blessings.

Fishkill and Green Haven

The night before reporting to Fishkill, my academy buddies and I crashed at a pay-by-the-night flophouse for transient staff near the facility. The owner, aptly nicknamed "Dirty Doug," lived up to his name, and his house was proof. Having grown up on a dairy farm that was known for being clean and orderly, these accommodations were, to me, not fit for humans. At a bagel shop that morning, I purchased a local paper and looked for places to rent. I called, got the details, and scheduled a showing for later in the day, after work. We immediately took the apartment and I roomed with my friend, Ron. He made it clear that he wanted to be my roommate because we were on the same page when it came to cleanliness.

Fishkill, despite being a medium-security facility, was complete chaos to me. Having been constructed in 1896 as the Matteawan State Hospital for the Criminally Insane, it was a large, sprawling facility. Inmates were everywhere, unescorted, and its layout was mind-boggling to the newcomer. The orientation was different from my Clinton orientation. We now were assembled with new officers from throughout New York State. Officers had attended the Penn Yan, Albany, and Harriman academies, as the system badly needed staff after a long hiring freeze.

There simply did not seem to be order to anything at Fishkill. The housing units seemed to be a maze, with no rhyme or rhythm to them. Nobody took the time to explain anything to you. At least Clinton had order and consistency. This was not my cup of tea. I followed the lead of my roommate and put in for a transfer to Green Haven Correctional.

Green Haven was a Maximum A-security facility, like Clinton. This was clearly where my comfort zone was.

Set in a quiet, country setting in Stormville, New York, Green Haven was a 20-minute drive from the apartment and it suited me just fine. I remained here until my transfer back to Clinton. This facility was the best representation of where I wanted to be: cells, walls, and order. It was also very dangerous.

I quickly caught on to the ways of Green Haven. The locals were taken care of and we transients got the leftover scraps of assignments. The very first Inmate Misbehavior Report that I issued to a Rastafarian inmate who stole food from the mess hall serving line was dismissed by the lieutenant at the disciplinary hearing. The report had been detailed and was perfectly written. I called Lieutenant Richardson, a tall, black man, and asked what I had done wrong and how the report could have been better. He told me the report was fine. So I asked why it was dismissed, to which he replied, "I believed him." I simply could not believe what I was hearing. It was very clear that some staff were a little too close to the inmates. Regardless, I was fascinated with the simple layout and the personalities it housed. These included inmates like the pleasant, but dangerous, short, Hispanic martial artist inmate named Poncho, who sported his Fu Manchu mustache, and a large, jolly, well-known inmate, nicknamed "Country," who was rumored to have a son playing college football. Another inmate who worked for me in the mess hall kosher kitchen was an Israeli named Daniel, a quiet, short, dark-haired, mustached man who always seemed to be sad. Others had told me that Daniel had been a restaurant owner who kept getting robbed. Daniel, being tired of criminals robbing him and his business, took matters into his own hands. During the last robbery, he pulled out his own weapon, got the drop on the robbers, and ordered them to drop their guns. When they did, he shot and killed them. Israeli justice, I guess. He worked alone as I supervised him. We had many pleasant conversations about his Israeli military service and life in his native country. Many years later, an inmate told me that Daniel had been released.

One inmate, in particular, was always quiet, polite, and respectful, but he gave off incredibly dark energy. His Departmental Identification Number, or DIN, told the tale. His bore an "H" designation. This letter indicated that he had been sentenced to death at one time when New York State had the death penalty. His sentence had since been commuted to life in prison without parole when the death penalty was overturned. This was his home... forever.

On one occasion I had the opportunity to tour the Death House. Our group made its way up and we looked at the dirty, old, abandoned area. The small yard was on the roof, with tall building walls around it, cells, and the electric chair. Some of the more morbid individuals took turns sitting in the chair and it weirded me out. I took notice of the writing on a wall where someone had written "Smith's Lawyer," with a number listed below it. Lemuel Smith was the inmate convicted of killing Officer Donna Payant in Green Haven in 1981. There was nothing more to serve as a reminder of those who had been housed there.

During my assignment as the Clinic Runner on the evening tour, other than escorting inmates for medication runs and emergency sick calls, part of my assignment was to respond to emergencies throughout the facility, if available. One evening, an emergency in the E and F Block yard was announced and I quickly responded. Upon arriving at the scene, I could see a large group of officers and staff attempting to surround one of the most popular inmates in the joint - Country! I quickly learned that an inmate had attacked and struck him with a weight bar and it did nothing to him other than piss him off even more. He'd begun to chase his attacker and probably would have killed him if staff had not intervened and surrounded him. The inmates in the yard were all yelling and screaming. Knowing that I could not be of assistance, I helped to keep the inmate bystanders away. Inmate Country was wild, screaming that he would exact his revenge. The sergeants and officers were safe until they placed their hands on him, then all hell broke loose. The entire yard erupted into a roar in protest. The inmates near me had been standing on the TV bleachers, but now it was a tidal wave of green as inmates began to make their way toward us. Beside me was a brand new Hispanic officer from the New York City area. He looked even younger than me and he was overtaken with fear. "What do we do?" he called to me. "Put your back to mine. Don't let anyone take your stick (baton)!" I called back. He did and we braced ourselves. At that very moment, I witnessed a miracle, much like I did when Sergeant Swanson stopped a fight with a simple touch and word. Country raised one of his huge arms, waved the inmates away, and called out, "Go back! I'll deal with this. Go back!" Everyone froze in place, but suddenly a rock struck a female sergeant in the head and down she went. More screaming and yelling from the inmates as I saw and heard an inmate close to me shout out, "Let the fat bitch die, kill her!" I was shocked because I immediately recognized the inmate as one of my former workers in the mess hall. When the issues were resolved, participants were identified and issued Misbehavior Reports. I wrote up my former worker and he received many months in the Special Housing Unit for inciting violence.

When the sergeant went down, the yard became much calmer. No inmate wanted to be associated with this assault. As the staff tried to carry her out, I ran ahead, alerted medical staff, and retrieved a gurney for her to be transported to the clinic area. She recovered from her injuries and retired years later as a Deputy Superintendent for Security.

The next assignment at Green Haven would be my last at that facility. I had chosen to take the position as the Protective Custody Unit Officer on the evening tour. I liked and appreciated working alone and being responsible for myself in the unit. This unit was located in A-Block and was secured by a door, then a gate. Nobody was allowed to enter without my opening the gate for them. It was my job to supervise the serving and cleanup of the evening meal, showers, and phone calls. The job was tough at first since I ran it by the book. This was difficult for the inmates to accept since the officer before me had been put into the job since his arrival at the facility just a few months prior. He'd run the unit loosely and allowed the cons to walk all over him. That all stopped when I took over.

One day, as I arrived in my unit, I was shocked to see an inmate's personal clothing hanging from the pipes that served as cranks to open and close the large cell block windows. I stopped in front of the clothing, trying to ascertain the owner. A voice meekly spoke to me from one of the cells, it was inmate Johnson. He was serving a life sentence for murder. The tall, thin, black con with the shaved head never spoke, other than when he would quietly and politely choose a phone time slot or if he wanted to take a shower. "Sir, those are mine," he said as he looked downward. He continued by saying, "Sorry, I thought it was your day off." I couldn't help but laugh and shake my head as I walked away and had his cell opened so he could collect his items. I was consistent and they knew what was expected of them.

The typical inmate in my unit was either a child molester, a rapist, a victim of extortion, an inmate unable to repay his gambling debts, or simply victim-prone. What was an unacceptable crime against women and children back in my early years in the department became the norm toward the end of my career. The department, a reflection of society, became flooded with them. I was always cautious to keep my life hidden from inmates. I never discussed my personal life with them, ever. However, the night that I left for my wedding, one of the inmates - a quiet, white guy from the Watertown area - stopped me as I passed by his cell. He said that he had something for me. Despite his always being polite and respectful, I immediately became suspicious and defensive as he produced a greeting card that all of the inmates had signed, congratulating me. Although it was a very respectful and sincere acknowledgment, it proved that the walls had ears and I would remember this lesson throughout my career.

A-Block in Green Haven ran pretty smoothly on the evening tour of duty. The A-2 Company was designated, "Mini-Segregation" and housed an overflow of SHU inmates. The officer and I had become good friends and handled our areas in a similar fashion: Firm, fair and consistent. He was a fellow northerner. The A-Block Second Officer was a local and was part of our cohesive unit. The only weak link was the First Officer. He was a short, stout, westerner who was too friendly, or "soft," with the inmates. On numerous occasions, I overheard him call inmates by their first name. One that particularly pissed me off was when I heard him refer to inmate Moseley as "Winston." This was the same repulsive Winston Moseley who had stalked, raped, and killed Kitty Genovese in 1964. Moseley was evil. He was creepy, rarely went to the yard, and never said a word to anyone. For him to have a relaxed relationship with one of us was alarming to say the least. One night, after witnessing yet another of this officer's rule violations, the three of us cornered him after the block was locked down for the night. We told him to either get with the program or find another post to work at. We did not want any heat from the administration for his antics. He listened and conceded that he was soft towards cons. He was aware that he needed to change his ways. I doubt that he ever did.

Another unusual inmate in A-Block was Larry Gordon. Gordon was a short, hyperactive man with a shaved head and glasses. Despite a 25-to-life sentence for murder in the 1970s, he had a toothy grin and was always willing to help out. I often teased him about sticking a candle in his ear to use him as a Jack-O-Lantern at Halloween. He was an inmate housed in the Intermediate Care Program or ICP, commonly referred to as the "Bugs." These inmates had mental defects of one type or another. Most were on heavy-duty medications and rarely caused problems, many of them quite child-like. Their program was also housed in A-Block.

On a quiet, warm, Sunday evening in October of 1989, Gordon and I were idly talking through the bars. There was something different that night and I will never forget what happened. Out of the blue, the inmate explained to me that he had gone to the Catholic services that morning. The priest had distributed scapulars to the inmates and he proudly pulled his from his pocket and showed it to me. He asked me if I knew what they were and I replied that I did. He handed it to me as he said, "This is the greatest gift that one man can give to another. I want you to have this." Catholics believe that anyone who has the scapular is assured of eternal life. I accepted this gift. Little did I know that I would be involved in a head-on automobile accident during my day off a few days later, on October 18, 1989, my parents' anniversary. According to anyone who had seen the wreckage, I should not have survived the accident. To this day I have no memory of what happened, but I still have that very same scapular in my wallet. I also bear the scars that remind me of that terrible day.

Back To Clinton – North Yard

While I was recovering, I received word that I was being transferred back to Clinton. I reached out to the staffing office and informed them that I was out until further notice. After recovering for over four and a half months, I convinced my doctor that I was fit for duty. Having hobbled daily in my attempts at running again, I still felt that I could defend myself. Awaiting for that day to arrive, I prepared my uniforms that had hung idly in the closet.

My reporting day arrived. The facility had changed hands from the last *warden* in New York State to its new *superintendent*, who had far less autonomy. I was sent to the staffing office, where I was greeted by a heavy-set, bearded senior officer and the tall Staffing Lieutenant with a booming voice. I was quickly assigned to an evening recreation job with a set RDO squad - Regular Day Off schedule and Vacation Letter. Having a set RDO squad was extremely beneficial, allowing me to make plans and adjust schedules indefinitely. If I had chosen to remain as a Resource Officer, I would have been bounced around from shift to shift, with my days off changing all of the time. The Resource Officers who were related to, drank with, or played sports with supervisors were often given preferential treatment. Since I had none of these very important qualifications, I elected to remain in the Recreation position. Vacation Letter schedules showed your vacation for years in advance. We were allowed to swap, turn in, or take a portion of the whole two-week vacation.

My routine at Clinton began. The daily challenge of finding a parking space on the hill outside the wall was usually a futile mission. I typically ended up hiking from what was referred to as the "North Forty." This was a remote overflow parking lot that was either plagued by mud or snow, depending on the season. On countless occasions, staff were forced to trudge through driving rain, snowdrifts, or sub-zero temperatures to and from that remote spot just to get to work. Upon checking in with the Assignment or "Chart" Sergeant and getting my winter uniform gear from my locker, I went off to lineup in the Blue Room. Gene Palmer, the same man that I used to work with as a laborer and now as a fellow Yard Officer, greeted me and gave me a heads-up regarding my assignments and duties.

The Chart Sergeant entered the room and we rose to our feet and loosely lined up on the rows of dark tiles, which greatly contrasted with the light-colored floor. The sergeant called out the supervisors on duty, read aloud any new memos, emergency response assignments, and did the roll call. The 2-10 tour of duty was mostly comprised of Yard, Gym, Bath House, Commissary, School and Law Library Officers. Upon being dismissed, we headed off to our assigned areas to provide hall coverage as the academic and vocational programs returned to their respective cell blocks. Once the halls were cleared, we headed to the North Yard.

The North Yard at Clinton is unique. Known as "Little Siberia," it truly lived up to its name. There is simply no other prison yard like it in the world. At one time, it had a ski jump, a ski run, and a skating rink. Overseen by officers in five armed wall posts, it is fenced off into three sections, with gates that could be secured and locked in seconds if an incident occurred.

These fences and gates were implemented after several incidents over the years. The upper level was where the basketball and handball courts were located, as well as the two televisions. The lower section was the ballfield where some very competitive football, softball, and soccer games were played. The middle section of the yard contained the courts. Courts were small pieces of property that inmates could possess with others. To prevent unauthorized use or theft, a registered member of the court was required to be present when other inmates were there. At no time could more than six inmates be on any court. Each court had its stove. Firewood was provided during the early yard on the weekends. The inmates would take the blocks of wood, haul them to their courts and split the wood by slamming or pounding the block onto a crude wood splitter – a 6-inch metal pipe with a sharpened edge sticking out of the ground. It was a method as effective as it was crude. The inmates were allowed to cook meals during their yard time. Enough food for a single meal was allowed to be brought out per yard session. On the weekend, they could bring enough for two. This was done so hoarding and stocking up for an uprising could not take place.

Many of the courts showed its inhabitants' pride of ownership. Birdhouses, painted stone walls, picket fences, and vegetable gardens were common. These courts offered a wonderful view of the Adirondack Mountains and the valley below. Tools were loaned out to the inmates so they could maintain their court and garden. It was an everyday occurrence to see inmates carrying shovels, rakes, hoes, hammers, and saws. It is kind of unnerving to see lifers with these tools going about their business. There always seemed to be a litter of kittens popping up, and the inmates would adopt and feed them. It is amazing how a little, helpless kitten can tame and soften even the hardest of criminals.

The phones were initially located in the old Phone Room. The room was simply lined with old type wood and glass door phone booths and the inmates could take turns using the phones based on the last two digits of their DIN number. For what seemed to be a very long time, I was assigned to the gate and controlled the flow. I can still hear myself saying, "00, 01, 02, 03, 04…."

Officers were assigned to any of the key ground posts or a roving patrol. Patrols would question suspected court trespassers, respond to incidents, or relieve ground post officers. The ground posts sat on elevated posts with a small roof, which afforded little protection from the elements. Spring would bring an attack by Adirondack black flies. Many of us would buy cheap cigars and puff away, keeping the nasty little bastards at bay. Summer would be hot and humid, with the stench of Jack Mackerel filling the air. "Jack Mack," as it was referred to, was an inexpensive fish that was readily available in the commissary. I don't think I will ever be able to forget that odor. Fall was beautiful as the valley and mountains slowly turned color and the crisp air and wood smoke hinted that winter was rapidly approaching. Winter was hell for the yard officers. The administration refused to give staff enclosures to protect us against the weather. We were forced to wear unauthorized personal clothing with our substandard, issued outerwear. This would be OK until we went back into the facility and we started sweating from all of the layers.

If the winter weather was deemed too extreme for the inmates, late recreation, after the 5:30 pm count, in the Mess Hall would be utilized. The inmates could use the phones in the Mess Hall, watch TV, play cards or some other games. Mess Hall recreation was utilized until the mid-1990s when the administration finally enclosed the ground posts and ran electricity to them with heaters. What a difference! Now it was the cons who were freezing while the staff members were nice and toasty.

I was fortunate enough to be on my days off the night the yard lights lost power. Even if they had immediately been turned back on, it would take time for them to provide sufficient lighting. The staff were pelted with rocks and it was a miracle nobody was hurt. There was no proper emergency lighting for such an incident. Shortly thereafter, handheld spotlights were installed in the yard wall posts. I was assigned to 12 Post when we lost power a second time. I snapped into action. I grabbed my rifle and the spotlight and scanned the area where the staff were. They notified me via radio that they were making their way to the recreation shack. This is where the loaned sporting equipment was issued to inmates. I replied that I had them covered. I continuously swept the region, identifying inmates in the area. It is highly unlikely that an inmate would even move, knowing that an alert officer was covering the area. None did.

During the time I was assigned to the North Yard and later, Clinton, as wells other facilities, suffered dramatic staffing changes. These job changes or eliminations altogether were fought long and hard but were implemented anyway.

Before their elimination in the early 90s, there were countless maintenance crews overseen by officers during the day. These crews did tasks throughout the facility. Paint crews painted everything from a company (gallery) of cells, a block, or other areas of the facility. We even had crews that scraped gum from the hallway floors and kept the place clean. Bit by bit, these jobs were eliminated, but the work still had to be done. I never agreed with the practice of allowing inmates to paint their own cells. This practice helped to facilitate the escape of two inmates from Elmira in 2003. A prudent move would have been to ban this practice statewide.

The closing of some armed wall posts on certain shifts or permanent closure of others left Clinton vulnerable. Following the escape in 2015, all wall posts were reopened.

The Church of Saint Dismas

Another unique feature of Clinton was the Church of Saint Dismas - The Good Thief. In the Catholic faith, Jesus Christ promised only one person eternal life, Dismas. While on the cross, Jesus said to him, "This day shalt thou be with me in Paradise."

Due to the persistence and perseverance of Father Ambrose Hyland, the Catholic priest at Clinton from 1937-1953, the Church of St. Dismas was built. Construction began in 1939 and was completed two years later, in 1941. This magnificent structure is located within the prison walls and its construction is well-documented in the book, *The Gates of Dannemora.* Tired of holding mass in the facility auditorium, which was under the mess hall, Father Hyland took on this massive project, which was placed on the National Register of Historic Places in 1991. With stone hewn from the prison grounds, beams from a barn, and Appalachian Oak donated by then-inmate mobster Lucky Luciano, craftsmen taught the inmates their trades. From stone cutting to carpentry, to stained glass, the work was all done by the inmates. Faces of inmates can be seen in these irreplaceable, handmade pieces of art. Two of the most impressive pieces within the church are the hand-carved planks from the ship of the explorer Ferdinand Magellan which were donated by one of Magellan's descendants.

The church was a peaceful and quiet place to work. Having only had the opportunity to be assigned there a few times in my career, I sincerely appreciated the history and explored it whenever the opportunity presented itself. The view of the Champlain Valley and Lake Champlain, with Vermont in the distance, was pleasant, but from the church tower, it was spectacular.

Since Clinton Main was divided into two parts, East and West, religious services were one of the few times that inmates from both sides of the facility were brought together. The West was comprised of A, Upper and Lower F, and Upper H Blocks. The East consisted of B, C, D, E, and the Hospital. Unfortunately, many of the inmates would try to attend mass in an attempt to engage in gang activity, smuggle contraband, or attempt to rendezvous with a homosexual lover. It was necessary to separate the groups from each other and space the inmates to minimize contact.

I do not ever recall any incident occurring within the church itself, but I do recall a few after services had ended and the inmates were being returned to their blocks. There was clearly respect for this masterpiece and an understanding that such behavior inside this holy place would not be tolerated by either side of the bars.

APPU

The Assessment and Program Preparation Unit - APPU - is housed in Lower H Block. The cleanest block in the facility, the inmates within this unit are typically victim-prone or infamous. Former cops, judges, correction officers, transsexuals, it was like a parade of circus sideshow attractions whenever they moved through the facility. Once the hall was secured by heavy metal gates, the show began. Of the more infamous and notorious inmates I encountered were Joel Steinberg, Joe Fama, rappers Tupac Shakur and Ol' Dirty Bastard, and serial killer Joel Rifkin, among countless others. People were amazed that I dealt with these men, and I always answered with, "They are cons. That's it." However, I took a very strong dislike to Rifkin. He was a highly-medicated, foot-shuffling monster with the most hideous laugh. I only had to tell him once to get away from me. It absolutely tipped me when an insanely liberal social worker in the Mental Health Unit was overheard saying that she was going to cure him. The same employee, I discovered, had been assisting an inmate with his legal case. The woman was nuts and clearly posed a danger to the departmental goals.

These inmates were here to stay, there wasn't another spot for them, so they chose to keep their home clean. Most had an education, some were financially secure and almost all of them were a pain in the ass. There seemed to be a higher degree of interaction between them, and some staff seemed to allow the separation between the con and officer to be narrowed. It was a spot ripe for a soft employee to be manipulated... and they were.

Liam Langley and Sam Bradley were some of those employees who opened themselves to being corrupted. Liam was an officer who was caught giving APPU parolees he knew rides to New York City and was allowed to resign rather than be terminated. Sam was an Assistant Deputy Superintendent who was allowing inmates to use his cell phone for a price. He also was allowed to resign. He was often seen stocking shelves at a local Walmart afterward.

As I was pat frisking a short, balding, older con from that block one day before he received a visit, he suddenly jumped and took his hands off the wall. I assisted him back into place and in a considerably less polite and professional manner than he was accustomed to, informed him that I was the wrong guy to do that to. He nervously apologized and was allowed to have his visit. One of the long-time, soft APPU officers who had escorted him to me pulled me aside and said, "You can't say that to him, he's a judge!" I had no clue who this con was, nor did I care. The officer went on to explain that he was in here for taking bribes.

Now I was seriously pissed off. "He was a judge, now he is just another con," I replied. A judge? Here was the one guy in life you were supposed to get a fair shake from and he is on the take. I should have just slammed his ass against the wall and done Use of Force and Misbehavior reports. I laughed like hell quite some time later while I was between shows at an amusement park: as I sat on a bench on a sunny day, I read the paper and instantly recognized the now ex-con, former judge in a news article, showing him packing items at a dress shop.

CERT

The Correction Emergency Response Team or CERT is comprised of officers who are trained for riot control, snipers, cell extractions, escape and pursuit, and anything else that they may be called upon to do. I had the privilege of being a member for several years and was later asked to apply for the Albany-based team, more commonly referred to as "Super CERT." This team was highly trained in all areas, including hostage rescue. I had the pleasure of training and becoming friends with some of the members in the mid-90s. Advanced CERT training was the best time of my career. Where else can you get paid to rappel off a building, shoot weapons, train with police agencies, and learn even more about the world of Special Operations in Corrections?

Many joined the team for the mission, others joined for the overtime pay - 4 hours a month - and it showed. I was on the evening tour, so I received no additional pay unless training took place on my night off. During the Y2K debacle, when inmates planned on initiating a work stoppage and other disruptive actions, many officers who had always bad-mouthed CERT became members just to suck up the extra pay. In the 90s there was a period when we were not even compensated whatsoever for training. Governor Mario Cuomo had slashed departmental budgets so drastically that we would either train on our own or not train. Many chose to stay away. Some of us trained anyway.

Four hundred plus CERT Officers marching into Washington Correctional Facility in the middle of the night was an incredible sight.

The author hanging from a building during Advanced CERT training

Teams from different regions had been brought together to regain control. Wearing bright orange jumpsuits, dark blue helmets with visors, gas masks on our hips, we marched with our fiberglass batons at port arms. The facility had an alarming number of incidents recently and Albany wanted to send the message that it would not be tolerated. We had been activated.

We took the dormitories by complete surprise. We rapped the beds of the sleeping cons and they awoke to a sea of officers in full riot gear. They nearly crapped themselves as they visibly shook with fear and they didn't dare make eye contact. The problematic individuals were identified and snatched from the area in the blink of an eye. No inmate wanted to be next. There was no mistaking who was in control now.

In 1996, convicted killer Darrell Brand escaped from the Clinton County Jail and I was part of that activation as well. The State Police were very thankful to have us working with them. One trooper disclosed to me, "You guys get more training in this than we do. We get it once in the academy and that's it." The incredible line of vehicles impatiently waiting to be searched began to flow and soon dwindled. One particularly difficult female driver tore into me, "Do you know who I am? I am Judge __________'s wife!" I carefully explained that her vehicle would indeed be searched and her compliance would expedite the process. She continued to spew venom but consented.

The most common task for CERT was cell extractions and Clinton had it down to a science. We had been recognized by Albany as the facility with the least amount of injuries and that fed right into the ego of one of the team leaders. As our true leader, Lt. Harry Corel was easing into retirement mode and his assistant, Lt. Brian McDonald was anxious to take the reins. Lt. McDonald liked to tell people that he had been a Navy SEAL, but it was all bullshit. Our new facility captain, Captain James Thomas, who was rumored to have been a strike of 1979 scab worker, wanted to see us in action.

Of the fifty officers present, he just had to pick me. "Blaine, suit up!" bellowed Sergeant Gerry Blake. I pretended not to hear him, for I was sitting in the back of the room, just like I had done for months. I had been seriously contemplating resigning from the team. My outside career was keeping me busy and I could no longer afford to risk getting injured. "Blaine, suit up!" he bellowed again. I rose from the antique, wooden all-in-one student chair desk and donned the gear. Inside the homemade, accurately furnished cell, Officer Ryan played the role of the inmate to be extracted. I was assigned as the second officer in the order to enter the cell. We were about to start the scenario when I stopped the action. "Where is our shield?" I asked. Lt. McDonald said, "It's broken, we are just simulating." I objected, "We should get one. We don't train without the proper equipment. Somebody's going to get hurt." "We are just simulating!" he countered. I again appealed to him, "We should send someone to get one from the arsenal. There are plenty there. It only takes a few minutes." "We are just fucking simulating!!" he yelled at me with the captain by his side.

We took Officer Ryan down hard and he struggled as we placed him into restraints. "Blaine, you go in first this time," Sgt. Blake directed, so I took my position. Officer Ryan had changed the scenario inside of the cell. He had used a blanket to prevent us from seeing inside. We could hear him moving items around the cell. Sgt. Blake relayed the info to me so I could be prepared. "Go, go, go!" he said, and away we went. I had my hands in the simulated position of holding a shield. Once I entered the cell, the officer threw a short locker at me, just like an inmate would do. Not having a shield to parry the object, I used my forearm to block, then I threw the locker to the left. I was forced to hold the locker back from striking other members and lose our momentum. My leather glove protected me from the sharp edges but suddenly I saw a flash of light and the most excruciating pain and warmth surged from my right thumb. The heavy, steel-barred cell door had just crushed my right thumb.

Having assisted once again with subduing the "inmate" and placing him into restraints, I exited the cell and moved to the back of the room. The most incredible pulsations and warm liquid feeling told me that this was bad. I slowly and gingerly pulled at the fingers of the glove as blood flowed out. Once the glove was removed, we could see the skin peeled back on the knuckle, the thumb kept twitching and bouncing around uncontrollably. I was taken to the local medical center in Plattsburgh where I received stitches, bandages and pain medication. This was the first

The author (left-center as part of the first New York Department of Corrections CERT Olympics Team in 1993

work-related injury that kept me out of work. My thumb is permanently injured with no improvement ever expected. Many officers, when they knew we were alone, would express their anger with that lieutenant. They were shocked that he would violate one of our cardinal rules about training without the proper equipment and 50 witnesses heard me object to his improper order. It wasn't long before he accepted a position as captain – a position that he had repeatedly turned down previously.

The CERT teams from Clinton and all over the state did an outstanding job in their search for inmates Matt and Sweat. They are to be commended for the long hours they worked in the nastiest of conditions imaginable and with failing equipment. Many retirees openly expressed their desire to be in on the search. I had no desire to be subjected to the conditions that these staff members faced: sun, heat, rain, humidity, and insects as they trudged through dense woods, swamps, and fields. Some retirees sought the glory, but all felt sympathy for the searchers.

Jailhouse Rumors

There simply are no secrets in prison. Nothing happens without us knowing, and I still insist that someone knew about the escape in 2015. Someone will go to their grave knowing that they received intel but did not lend the information any credibility. Escape from Clinton? Impossible!

Informants are always providing information for a multitude of reasons, usually self-serving. Staff informed on other staff as well, and everyone loved a good rumor. It didn't matter if it was credible or not, people simply loved the gossip. No matter what someone had done, it would be forgotten as soon as someone else committed an equally or greater inane act. One day, I said to a friend that we could create the most ludicrous, unbelievable rumor and whisper it into the wind from the front gate and it would be carved in stone by the time it got to C Block.

People do stupid things and some of the Clinton supervisors were living proof of it. One such moment concerned a lieutenant who strutted about with a holier-than-thou attitude and, in an extremely weird manner, greeted people with "Howdy." He loved to target staff members from his office rather than try to assist them. He always chose the wrong side of an argument and it usually ended up with the union fighting him and having it rammed up his backside in a most humiliating fashion. These defeats would spread like wildfire throughout the facility and he would once again look like the incompetent fool that he was. One of the few times that I ran into him and his very attractive wife was in a store located in Plattsburgh. He introduced us and she bubbled and was so incredibly friendly that I actually felt sorry for this asshole, who just stood there with the personality of a damp dishtowel. I just could not see the personalities meshing... it didn't click.

It didn't take long for my suspicions to be confirmed: there were issues at home. The facility was abuzz over the latest rumor, that the same lieutenant was allegedly caught with a female civilian staff member who was supposedly in lingerie in their office, after regular hours, when a maintenance worker walked in. A retired administrator told me years later that not only had the incident happened, but that he was forced by the superintendent to pay the overtime that this moron had the audacity to request. The incident had been whitewashed, despite an investigation by the Inspector General. The rumor was reinforced when Lieutenant "caught-with-his-pants-down" showed up for work wearing sunglasses, sporting a few noticeable marks, including a black eye that strongly suggested that his playmate's husband had become aware of the situation and taken matters into his own hands - literally. The lieutenant was clearly out of his league. I do not recall a single employee feeling bad for him, ever, not even when his wife left him years later and took him to the proverbial cleaners. By that time, he was a captain and I was a lieutenant, and I was forced to listen to his woes daily. I was going through an amicable divorce, complete with a prenuptial agreement. It drove him nuts that I walked in each day with a smile and happy. Why not? I was still relatively young, successful, and approaching retirement. As they say, he was so broke that he couldn't afford to even pay attention. Since he lived in state housing, he didn't even own the proverbial pot to pee in or window to throw it out of. I was living large and his life sucked. It still does to this day.

I later learned of a rumor that "Captain Caught" had a crush on a former employee. I would later receive confirmation. He clearly must have accessed confidential employee information and started calling her, which freaked her out. Mary was a beautiful, fun and lively counselor who explained that she did not like the captain in a romantic way and told him so. I wonder if he greeted her with "Howdy!" The guy clearly had issues.

I was often asked by fellow staff members why people would feed into rumors and outright lies. I would sit them down and simply explain to them:

The vast majority of the people that we work with have nothing to show for their existence. They're jealous. They will never be happy, for others who are doing better than they are. Lies are like a painting. You take a blank canvas and draw whatever you desire. You can color it in any manner that you wish. The truth is black and white and it will never change. It simply isn't as appealing. That is why people choose lies and rumors over the truth. The truth just does not appeal to their senses the way a rumor does.

A few times in my career, some people just needed a reality check. One, in particular, was a poorly educated, backwoods, dim-witted officer, Tim Brault. Tim never heard a rumor that he didn't like. The only problem was that he wasn't bright enough to disseminate the information or to verify it. One evening, he chirped a comment as I passed by. I stopped, placed the items I was carrying on the floor and squared off.

"Let's go!" I challenged him.

He nervously said, "Oh no. I just wanted to get ya going."

"Well, ya got me going, now let's see if you're man enough to handle it!" I replied, but he refused to engage. He knew there was no way he could handle it. The officer controlling the gate was one of the nicest, yet toughest men to work there, confiding in me after that I had, most effectively, put Tim in his place. He knew he would get his ass kicked and he wasn't stupid enough to try that again. This same statement proved to be true time and time again. After I retired, I learned the truth about so many of my former co-workers and their lives. I feel sorry for anyone who works their career in such a place and has so little to show for it.

I remember a gorgeous day when Lana, a Mental Health RN, who was clearly upset, walked into my area, leaned on the window, obviously troubled, and finally spoke. She asked me, "Why? Why are people here so mean?"

I put on my hypnotherapist cap and asked her, "What are you doing right now?"

She looked at me oddly and said, "I am looking out the window."

I then explained to her how things and our environment subconsciously affect us. She asked me to explain. I walked her through how when she woke up she was not allowed to get all made up and dress nicely. Here they had to dress down. She drove up and was greeted by wire and a wall with armed posts.

I continued by explaining that she parked, walked along the ominous wall, waited to be buzzed through the steel and reinforced glass door, showed an ID, went through a controlled gate and was buzzed through another door and she wasn't even to the administration building yet! Together we counted the gates and obstacles. I reminded her that everyone wore uniforms, stripped of originality or independent thought. Now she was leaning on a steel window frame with reinforced glass, looking through steel bars and past a wall with more wall posts. All of this to enjoy that wonderful view of the Champlain Valley, Lake Champlain, and the Green Mountains of Vermont. I explained to her that once you were aware of all of the negativity bombarding you, it was easy to ignore it and watch others be consumed by it. We discussed it a bit more, then she left my area smiling. One less miserable employee that day.

Talents and Personalities

The staff at Clinton possessed some of the most unique talents ever assembled in one facility. Some of them, the very best in their trade, wore blue uniforms eight hours and fifteen minutes a day.

Early one evening, a sergeant and two officers had transported an inmate from Shawangunk Correctional, and they were clearly confused as they prepared to leave the parking lot in front of the facility. They kept looking up towards the front gate area and gawking as the officer inside the wall post was marching about. "Can I help you guys?" I asked.

"What the hell is that sound?" he asked as he looked around.

"That's Gary, he's a bagpiper and he's practicing on his chanter," I informed him. The sergeant and his men were amazed.

"What kind of place is this?" he asked. I explained to him that within the wall were some of the best artists, loggers, farmers, carpenters, carpet layers, plumbers, electricians, masons, mechanics, and entrepreneurs of all sorts. He shook his head in amazement.

"I'm a hypnotist," I added. This was simply too much for him to absorb. "We gotta get the hell outta here!" he said to his men and they sped away.

Those who realized and utilized their wonderful talents were very pleasant to work with. We knew how to get things done, and we did. Not everyone was as fortunate. We had a balance, work ethic, and lifestyle that others just could not comprehend. Nobody had given us anything; we had earned it! While we were investing our time, talent, and money into a project, they were busy getting drunk and telling lies about the deer they have killed or the women they slept with. Karma bit one of these drunken womanizers in the ass, and in a huge way. Mark Dashnaw was married to a very nice girl I had gone to school with. For years, I had to bite my tongue as he had numerous affairs out in the open. It had not gone unnoticed by his wife, because Mark was livid when he discovered that she was having an affair of her own! Everyone was laughing at him behind his back as what went around simply came around.

Many staff members were just plain miserable and ignorant. Not unlike high school, they tried to hide their shortcomings by focusing attention on others and ridiculing them. Some people were just incapable of being truthful or pleasant. Some, like Brandon Adams, preferred to tell lies about his wife, their kids and the beautiful house they owned. The truth, when finally revealed, was that he and his girlfriend lived in the basement of her parent's house with her kids. Other staff were fine one-on-one but became "Instant Assholes - Just Add Audience," as I liked to say. It was laughable to see the lineup room unknowingly segregated into little groups or clicks: volunteer firemen, sports gamblers, hunters, and snowmobilers. The guys who owned and rode sleds were relentless as they wove their tales of bull. Each day brought new boasts and brags. It completely soured me on ever owning a snowmobile. The hunters spun their tales of big kills, leaving us careful to not step into bullshit or slip on the imaginary "gut piles" all over the floor.

Alcohol consumption seemed to be just part of the routine. After all, in the academy, there were daily references to it by the instructors. Every party or event exposed the issues some employees had with it as well. Some employees simply could not hide it. More than one has slept it off on duty while others covered their duties for them. One, in particular, was Ross Dobbs, more commonly referred to as "Otis." This reference was to the town drunk on the TV comedy *The Andy Griffith Show*. Otis would, without fail, get drunk and make his way to the sheriff's office and sleep it off in a cell. Ross wasn't all that different. He was a night tour officer who came to work drunk after his bowling league nights. The watch commander was tired of his antics, so he told him not to come to work on those nights. Ross obtained swaps with guys on my shift and the miserable, worthless asshole would be forced upon us.

Ross would make his way to the second floor of the old hospital with a bad attitude and no desire to fulfill his duties. We would often call out, "Lock in Otis!" He would look for a chair in the hospital mess hall, close the door, and close his eyes. It was laughable when he needed a liver transplant years later. They were going to give this guy a new liver? Seriously?

One unfortunate alcohol-related death was that of a female officer, Felicity Baker. Despite the considerable education she possessed, she had many issues. On what seemed like countless occasions, she came to work intoxicated, even falling in front of inmates. The administration refused to pull the proverbial trigger, discipline her, and hopefully wake her up enough to seek help. Years later, she was discovered dead in her driveway. I have often wondered that if there had there been a consistent application of discipline applied, would she be alive today?

One person I admire to this day is Ray Farley. Ray had been an Army paratrooper when he was younger. A damn good husband and family man, but it all fell apart. Ray found solace in booze and one bad thing after another turned his world upside down. I worked with him a great deal over the years and watched him hit the bottom, rock bottom, go through rehab, and get his life back together. One thing about Ray is that he always did his job. He has been sober now for over 15 years. If this man can do it, anyone can. It is always a pleasant reunion when we see each other.

Some of the staff were odd, but they provided seemingly endless entertainment. Ida was a nurse who worked with us but wasn't as old as she looked. She was going through a late mid-life crisis and was constantly getting tattoos. She had something for Ronnie Sandberg, an older bachelor with a seemingly endless amount of knowledge and an incredibly dry wit. One day Ronnie confided in me that Ida kept trying to show her latest tattoo to him. He was trying to keep her at bay. I told him to simply suggest that she get a picture of John Wayne tattooed on her ass. He asked me why would he ever suggest that. I said that if she asked why, he should tell her, "There's nothing like a western on the big screen." We laughed together and continued the small talk. However, I know he never used that line.

Cons and Lawsuits

Almost nobody gets through their career without being sued by an inmate. Why not? After all, liberals have empowered these poor, helpless criminals and offer them everything they need: a law library, complete with trained inmate law clerks, forms, sympathetic judges and juries are all theirs for the taking. It costs them nothing to do so once they have applied for indigent status. From melted ice cream to completely fictitious accusations of abuse, nobody was safe from this legal form of harassment.

"Go to the Legal Office," Sergeant Lowell told me one day as I checked in for my tour. I signed for my copy of a lawsuit and representation by the Attorney General. The story of physical abuse and theft by myself against this poor inmate was nearly a complete fairy tale. The only true part was that I had escorted the inmate with a group of other inmates as they returned from the commissary. I had done it as a favor for the Commissary Officer after I had secured my tailor shop inmates in Upper H Block.

"I knew we had this case won within 10 seconds of you stepping into the room," said Don Hanson, my attorney from the AG's office. "You are oozing with credibility," he added. We were headed to federal court. The inmate initially wanted $80,000 but was now willing to settle for $400. No dice.

The night before the trial was to start, I met with the attorney to begin preparations. "I just don't get it," I told him. "If you were to ask the jurors if they have ever been stopped by a cop for speeding or some other infraction and been given a break, would you sue them? Hell no, you would be appreciative. I know I am!"

"You know, I'm going to use that!" he said, as he scribbled on his pad. We were ready to roll tomorrow.

The legal process is pretty entertaining. Just like he said he would, my attorney polled the jury regarding being given a warning from a cop. Only one juror out of the entire pool had never received a break on a ticket. Our jurors were selected and the trial began. The plaintiff's case was presented. The inmate started right out of the gate by lying about his criminal history. It is pretty darn near impossible to sit in a suit in federal court and be forced to maintain your composure. To hear lie after lie being told about you; to have a single, subjective word in a performance evaluation from 1989 being beaten to death, objected to, and beaten some more in an attempt to discredit or humiliate you makes your blood boil.

I began to watch the jury. I saw the movements that they made and saw what they were and were not interested in. I began to pace and mirror them and attempted to develop an unconscious rapport with them. There was one female juror, a middle-aged blonde woman I just could not get a read on; she was tough. The plaintiff's line of crap was done and we started the defense. Our first witness was the 1st Officer of the Block, an employee I never trusted and who allowed this inmate free access to catwalks and other areas of the block with tools. He did this even after I informed him of the inmate's history of escape. Next was the sergeant who was in the area at the time. He was excitable and all over the place. Day one was done.

The next day the physician assistant who'd seen the inmate for his alleged injuries gave his testimony. He was a solid, knowledgeable, impressive witness. I had worked with him for years but I now saw him in a much different light. The witnesses were done testifying and the attorney and I were headed to lunch. I was to testify when we resumed.

"I am afraid this is going to bite us in the ass," he said. I asked him what he meant. He explained that typically the defendant testifies and the witnesses corroborate. We were doing it backwards because we simply could not get all of the witnesses together on the same date. Now I was to testify and it appeared that we were tailoring my testimony to corroborate theirs.

"You're fine," I told him.

He cocked his head to the side and asked in nearly an insulting tone, "And you know this how?" he asked. He simply wasn't ready for my reply.

"I have spent two days watching the jury. I've been pacing and mirroring them." He was puzzled as I laid out for him each jury member's behaviors. I had to admit to him that I just simply could not get a good read on the one blonde. She was a tough one. The look on his face was priceless. He now thought that he had a lunatic on his hands.

My testimony was clear and direct. I corrected the misleading information the plaintiff and his attorney had presented. I also had a little bit of fun at the expense of the court-appointed attorney for the inmate. It probably wasn't fair, but I noticed that the guy would lose his place whenever an objection was made and the argument presented. If the judge sustained the questioning, I would simply ask the attorney to repeat the question and he would stumble, flip through pages, and spit and sputter as he struggled to find his place. He looked like a fool every time.

The testimony was done. The jurors left the room to deliberate. They could easily be heard laughing and carrying on. About 45 minutes later, they were brought in. I was found not guilty. My attorney asked the judge if we might speak with the jurors and he said yes.

"What did you like about our case?" he asked. Two female jurors, one being the hard-to-read blonde, spoke up. They said that the inmate was a lying piece of crap, had tried to mislead them, and I did a great job correcting them. They liked our witnesses and laughed about the sergeant screwing up.

Then the blonde dropped a bomb on my attorney. "You asked us all of these questions, can we ask him some questions?" she asked as she pointed to me. He asked if I wanted to answer them and I said that I would. "Are you married?" she asked.

The attorney, a tall, stout man, doubled over laughing. He finally caught his breath and bellowed, "Wait 'til I call your superintendent. We didn't have the better case, we won because you're a stud muffin!"

We went across the street for a drink. The man who only a few hours earlier thought that I was completely out of my mind was now asking me to explain this science to him. I walked him through it and he was now fascinated.

Assaults and Use of Force

There are two types of force: physical force and deadly physical force and I utilized both during my career. Very few people will ever experience the feeling of realizing that something bad was about to happen in a maximum-security prison, much less the responsibility to act. Prisons are routine, so it is pretty obvious when the atmosphere becomes thick with tension and eerily quiet. You visually scan the yard or mess hall to see where the inmates are looking, then wait. The odds are never in your favor. Relatively few people will experience doing chest compressions on a body going cold beneath them. A greater number will experience having human feces thrown onto them. Countless employees throughout the department have, and I am one of them.

Not only is it disgusting, inhumane, and vile, it is the ultimate in degradation. It has long-lasting, if not permanent, effects on the victim. We may forget an appointment, a birthday, or what we had for dinner last night, but we never forget these and other horrific events as well as the assaults upon us. Some manage it better than others. I have never spoken to anyone other than fellow staff about many of the incidents that I was involved in. The public would simply never understand. There is no way that they could comprehend the madness. They could never accept that we could eat a bowl of chili as we watched a stabbing victim bleed, or joke as the facility doctor or physician assistant sewed up the cheek of a victim who fell victim to an assailant with a razor blade.

Most of the violence in Clinton was in the North Yard. From the moment that they arrived via a draft bus, the inmates were told that fighting in the blocks, mess halls, gym, auditorium, and shops would not be tolerated. If they had an issue with another inmate, they were to deal with it in the yard. With the five armed wall posts to provide coverage from above, we would give them enough time to handle it, but it was over when we said it was over. When we ordered them to stop, it was finished.

I was fortunate to be under the watchful eye of Jim Slater in 8 Post. Jim was a kind, older officer who had justifiably shot several inmates over the years. Once he'd shot an inmate with a rifle as he was stabbing another. Another instance was when he'd used the shotgun to keep back a massive storm of inmates from rushing the yard door. I loved and appreciated this man's judgment. He would sit and watch behind his dark, wrap-around sunglasses.

One day in 1993, while working the 9:45 am-5:45 pm tour, I was escorting porters with the property I had just packed in E-Block. We were approaching the gate, which led to the administration building, when the emergency tone sounded over the facility radios: "Level Two, North Yard. Level Two, North Yard."

It was only a moment later when the radio came to life again: "All available help report to the yard!" I then saw staff of all ranks, including captains and assistant deputy superintendents, racing to respond. Knowing it was something big, the officer at the gate took control of my inmates and I responded. It was a bad day… very bad.

As I approached the yard door, the officer posted there informed us that an inmate had been shot as he'd stabbed an officer. Batons in hand, we entered the yard and saw the inmate's blood on the ground. Inmate Leroy Dewer, who had been involved in the 1971 Attica riot, had quickly fashioned a weapon out of a rolled-up can lid and toothbrush. He'd stabbed the officer from behind and was shot by the officer in 8 Post as he'd chased the first officer. The officer survived the attack and Dewer was sent to the local hospital. I was present as he was loaded into the ambulance, moaning in pain.

The facility was shut down for a few hours until the administration could determine if this was an isolated incident. Every inmate was escorted within the facility that day with our batons in hand and their hands behind their head. The machine had roared to life.

Although I had worked wall posts on countless occasions, it was June 29, 1998, while working 12 Post, that I first fired a warning shot. The incident began as a simple fight and I stepped out on my catwalk, rifle in hand. As I stood with my weapon in a high port position, the situation began to evolve. The stabbing type motions of one inmate changed everything and I charged my weapon. With two fingers, I had quickly pulled and released the charging handle, stripping a round from the box-type magazine into the chamber, and watched.

The inmates took off on a run and started to fight again. One inmate broke away and began to run through the courts as I yelled in futility, "Stop!" He began to run up the hill walkway, unaware that he was running to his death. From my vantage point, I could see that it was like tossing a pebble into a pond. A few Hispanic inmates started, then more, then what seemed like all of them headed for this one guy. "He's dead!" I said aloud.

Without any mental debate, instinct and training took over. In a flash, I had flipped off the safety, pulled up my weapon, and I suddenly realized that I had just discharged my firearm.

"Get on the ground!" I began to yell. The inmates were confused as to which wall post had fired the warning and began to get down. The other four wall post officers were now out with their weapons, shouting commands as well. My mind began to race as I kept saying over and over, "I know I'm right. I know I'm right..."

My phone in the tower began to ring nonstop. I refused to let myself be distracted. My radio crackled to life: "Control to 12 Post, answer your phone!"

I did and Sergeant Lowell demanded, "The watch commander is on the phone with Albany. They need to know where you fired that round."

My response was textbook/lesson plan perfect, "In my pre-determined safe area over the church."

"Gooooood fuckinnnnngggg answer!" he said and the phone went dead.

To this day, I can still feel that rifle in my hands, see the sights, and hear the buffer spring as I fired that round. I guess it will always be there, just like the remnants of so many other incidents, such as assisting the medical team by doing chest compressions on a body going cold.

The investigator from the Inspector General's office showed up the next day. Armed with my documentation, my union representative and I headed upstairs. The incredible arrogance of the investigator was beyond belief. "I don't have a problem with what you did," is how he started our interview.

My rep was reading my mind when he challenged him, "Have you ever fired a non-training round on duty?"

The investigator admitted that he had not and we began. He asked me what had happened and I read my report. He asked me if I could tell him without reading it and I admitted that I could. I could because I had memorized it…word for word. He rolled his eyes, dropped his pen onto the table and said, "You're fine. Get out of here."

When an officer miraculously survived being stabbed repeatedly in Upper H Block, the Clinton machine roared to life again. The staff insisted that the administration reinstate a long-removed rule of no talking in the corridors. The administration had no real choice but to support this rule and reinstate it. Several incidents occurred because of its re-implementation, as inmates initially resisted, but it still stands today.

Tailor Shops

I was always suspicious of civilian staff who worked closely with inmates with no officers present. Many times these staff members despised security staff and sided with cons behind the scenes. I was always even more suspicious when I worked the tailor shops on the evening tour and the tall, red-headed female civilian supervisor needed to take an inmate from one area to another, unsupervised. My co-worker was assigned to another shop and we would call one another to "clock" them, the amount of time to get from one place to another, just to make sure nothing improper was happening. We spoke with our watch commander about these constant interruptions and he said he agreed, but it was allowed.

The inmates appreciated their industry jobs. If their academic and vocational needs had been met, they were eligible for an assignment to the shops. If not, they were assigned to a school or vocational program. When I was a lieutenant later on in my career, I always enjoyed the Program Committee and giving the security input regarding assignments. I always knew which officers could handle the less than motivated, or difficult, inmates. I would always call them and give them a heads up. Almost always, I would hear the voice on the other end of the line start chuckling with "No problem, Mike!"

Sometimes the industrial representative on the panel would try to persuade security staff to assign some inmates to certain shops. I absolutely refused to assign a sex offender or outright rapist to any location where there would be one-on-one contact with female staff. It just did not make sense to do it, regardless of their qualifications. It was this type of behind-the-scenes interference by civilians that kept inmates Matt and Sweat in the tailor shops.

Each shop had different functions. Materials were received and stored in the Industrial Stockroom. Tailor 5 would roll out layer after layer of cloth. Patterns were traced and the cloth pieces cut. The assigned shops would receive the pieces and sew them together. The items would then be moved to the final stop for packaging the finished products. Each shop was supervised by a civilian who oversaw the training and production by the inmates, and an officer who oversaw the security of the shop. The desks of the two were no more than a few feet from one another on the platform in any of the shops. Security and industrial supervisors made rounds daily and signed the logbook.

When Joyce Mitchell and her family claimed that she had felt endangered and that she'd had to engage in her illegal dealings with inmates Matt and Sweat, many people I met expressed sympathy for her until I set the record straight. You could see the looks on their faces turn into disgust as I explained the shop layout and how all she had to do was notify a single individual of what was transpiring. Her duties would not have allowed her to be inside the main facility, other than the administration building. Had she told anyone of the impending escape or the sexual advances by inmate Matt, the con would have been snagged, bagged, and transported to another facility within a few hours so the investigation could reveal the facts. She would have undoubtedly been allowed to resign rather than face messy and embarrassing criminal charges, and she would've been little more than a footnote in Clinton's history.

The state dropped the ball when investigating allegations of misconduct involving Mitchell and the two inmates. Standard operating procedure involves searching the inmate's living quarters and in this case, the work area. This was never done.

I have to admit that I was never aware of Gene Palmer's activities in the facility. As a supervisor, I had a reputation for not tolerating bullshit, and he and I never discussed anything other than exchanging pleasantries as I signed his overtime sheets. After the escape, I was asked to be a character witness for his defense and I was questioned by his attorney regarding his actions. I was open and honest and admitted that I had no knowledge of Gene's actions in the facility. I was asked if I was aware of his involvement in providing information to the administration and I admitted that I was not. Officers do not conduct investigations. They simply provide tips and info to superiors, who process and move the information onward.

OBS-1

The greatest education I have ever received in my life was OBS-1. This observation unit consisted of seven rooms. Over the years, many people have referred to this part of a facility as the "padded" or "rubber" room. Having worked Clinton's OBS-1 for many years, let me assure you there is no padding. It is a simple room with concrete walls, a steel-screened, barred-window, and a steel bed. Depending on their status, the typical inmate was given two thin mats to lay on, or cover with a thin paper gown. The less you give someone, the less chance of them hurting themselves. The whole unit had an odor that could not be scrubbed away.

I appreciated the relative quiet of OBS. Over the years, my duties included the admission and discharging of inmates, feeding, and rounds throughout the evening at 15-minute intervals. The downtime between rounds allowed me to conduct my personal business, read, or pursue any other activities I was involved in. I always received compliments on how clean and quiet this unit was when I was working. I was often jokingly accused of hypnotizing the inmates there. Although I never entranced them, I did use my non-verbal and indirect verbal skills to calm them at times. When I was away, others would demonstrate less interest in the cleanliness and behavior of the inmates housed there.

In that unit, I had housed and dealt with some of the nastiest human beings God ever put on Earth. No matter who I dealt with, I treated them the same and gave each one this speech when they were admitted:

Whatever you did before this very moment is on you. I am going to judge you from how you conduct yourself from now. If you conduct yourself like a man, I will treat you like a man. If you say yes sir, no sir, please and thank you, you will get everything you are entitled to and probably a little bit more. Should you conduct yourself less than human, I will treat you less than human. I will now leave you with these words: Never bite the hands that will feed you.

When maintenance would spray for roaches upstairs in the hospital second-floor area above OBS-1, it would drive them to my area, and the walls and floor would come to life. Once, an inmate from another facility arrived. I met him at the door. I warned the con that where he had come from was a whole lot better than where he was going. He refused to heed my advice and spewed off all kinds of vulgarities. After his interview with the mental health nurse, he was escorted to me for admission. When he saw the room where he was to be kept, he stopped dead in his tracks, his jaw dropped and he gasped, "I have to stay here?" He could see the walls and floor literally moving with roaches. Within minutes of being admitted, he conceded that I had warned him. He was repentant and wanted to take any housing assignment he was given. I told him that he was screwed for the night but tomorrow morning OMH (Office for Mental Health) staff would interview him. The next afternoon, when I came on duty and made my initial round, it revealed one very happy inmate who had been discharged and awaited his ride back to his facility. I asked him to tell all of his buddies about his experience. It would cut down on the number of inmates pretending to be crazy and wanting a change of scenery for a few days. It worked.

Some inmates would listen and heed my words, others would not and learned the hard way. The rapper Ol' Dirty Bastard, aka ODB, was a nasty, miserable prick who lived up to his stage name. Needless to say, we did not get along very well. Kenneth Kimes, the son portion of the mother & son grifter team who were convicted in the death of 82-year-old Irene Silverman, spent 19 days with me. This was following his taking a Court TV reporter hostage in the South Visiting Room back in October 2000. Once he was taken down, he was brought to me, where I admitted him and gave him the speech about his conduct. He refused to acknowledge me and we secured the room. He glared at me every time I made my 15-minute rounds. He had pure, unadulterated hate and death in his eyes. It wasn't until his third day with me that Kimes spoke to me in a civil tone. It was clear that he needed something and he was forced to be cordial. I listened to his request and informed him that I could indeed fulfill it. I then asked him why he suddenly changed. His response was simple, yet direct: "Sir, I have come to realize that you are my lifeline." I nearly laughed out loud, but the last thing I wanted to do was humiliate him. Humble, yes. Humiliate, no.

I have witnessed Mental Health administer medications to bring inmates from insane rages down to controllable levels. Many times the injections seemed to knock them out for a few days. I have also dealt with some of the evilest, destructive men who would try and lure you and other staff into the use of force just to liven up their day. One of these men was named Bermudez. He was a mean, miserable asshole doing life, but I had his respect. I refused to lie to him. It started one day when he asked me a question and I told him the truth. It wasn't what he wanted to hear and he went into a rage. I explained to him that I had nothing to gain from lying to him. However, if he would tell me exactly what he wanted me to say, I would recite it for him, adding my own disclaimer that it was a lie. I told if he wanted lies that he should ask someone else. I had nothing to gain by lying to a man in a cage. "You're right, Blaine," he said, "you're right." We never had an issue after that. Our paths would cross again a few years later at another facility.

Some inmates needed to be reasoned with in other ways. One big, muscle-bound black inmate had been determined to lash out whenever he could. There simply was no reasoning with him. Hour after hour, he attempted to get under my skin, then he crossed the line. I had always told cons that this wasn't personal, it was simply business. This guy wasn't having any of it. He was angry and he hated everyone and everything. Finally, I'd had enough and told him that in 20 minutes I was coming in and that I was going to ask him to repeat what he had said.

"You're not coming in here," he said.

"Like hell I'm not," I replied.

"You aren't coming in alone," he challenged.

"You're right," I countered. "I never said that I was coming in alone. You see, a man has to know his limitations and I'm not too proud to ask for help. There isn't one of you that ten of us can't lick. I will never lose!"

Knowing that his behavior would no longer be tolerated and that I indeed had the upper hand, he said, "That's the way it's going to be?" I informed him that was exactly how it was going to be. Although it was tense dealing with him, after that he knew he had played his hand.

Other inmates were truly crazy; they would run headfirst into a door or wall, climb up onto their toilet/sink unit and leap onto the floor. Others would simply play in their waste. One morning, a group of fresh-faced trainees arrived and were being shown around. I was asked to explain the function of my unit and my duties. I escorted the new officers down the hallway and informed them that I had a very talented artist in room number 7. As we passed by, they all strained to see inside, but I stopped them before they got too close. "That isn't chocolate pudding on that window!" They jumped back and started gagging. Yes, it was crap-covered, just like the walls in his room.

The skills that I developed there as an officer would benefit and serve me well for the duration of my career. In addition to the skills I possessed from my personal life, it was easy for me to read a person's energy, pick their body language apart or dissect their speech patterns.

Clinton in General

Cons preferred Clinton to most maximum-security prisons because they knew their place with staff. Although we would joke and interact, we could also roar with ferocity when necessary. On several occasions, they would speak of how facilities differed, which ones they liked, disliked, and why. The nonstop tension in one facility, the seeming steroid injected staff at another, each place had a personality or a flavor.

On a clear night, the lights of Clinton and the village of Dannemora were visible from points in Vermont more than 38 miles away. It became the home to some of the more notable inmates. If a crime made the news, we could expect to see the accused someday as an inmate. Some newsmakers in their day still called Clinton their home when I was an officer there. Robert Bongiovi had been the bodyguard for organized crime member Joey Gallo. Bongiovi was a pleasant, cordial porter in B-Block. Joseph "Mad Dog" Sullivan was a very quiet, yet deadly man and spent a great deal of time in the SHU under Administrative Segregation status. One inmate who always made his presence known was Harold Konigsberg. This inmate was as loud as he was big. Allegedly, he used to hold his victims by their ankles as they dangled outside the windows of a building. He would always try to make demands and test boundaries with staff. You would never think that this fat, old man with a temper was dangerous. That is until you saw his fists fly. I did and I am still shocked by what I saw.

Konigsberg was in the North Yard and the other inmates were lined up on the flats, waiting to be called in. One group after another would be escorted in when directed over the yard PA system. A young inmate was joking with Konigsberg and was playfully jabbing him. It was clear that the old mobster had some life left in him as his fists began to fly. Intentionally not hitting the younger inmate, his fists were a blur. The old man taught that kid a huge lesson and I laughed as I watched. Had he wanted to beat up the kid, the kid would have been the seriously bloodied loser of the bout. Amazing!

The clearest example of inmates knowing when Clinton roared to life was in the cell blocks. Each block has a PA System, with a microphone at the 1st Officer's desk for block announcements. As porters moved about the block completing their assignments or waiting idly on a company near the officer's cage, they would shuffle off to their cells with the announcement, "Porters on the cells." If an incident in the block or a Level II emergency within the facility was announced, the tone and message would change to, "Porters on the cells, now!" This simple change would have the inmates looking for a hole to crawl into.

Built on the side of a mountain, Clinton is stairs, stairs, and more stairs. I knew of four of us who had hip replacements in 2017 alone. The place just beat the hell out of your joints. An employee's duties could have them starting their day in one part of the facility and ending up on the other side with repeated trips to the mess hall, hospital, or elsewhere. More than once, an emergency in C-Block would be announced while I was at the farthest point away.

Over the years, the administration, likely at the direction of the Central Office, did some dangerous things to cut their spending. The most dangerous, idiotic move ever was the closure of the secured unit at the local outside hospital. This small unit kept all of the bad apples in one barrel, away from civilians. The administration directed that an inmate would be one-on-one with an unarmed staff member. With no officer assigned as an armed "rover" to assist and relieve staff, we were told to

An ariel view of the Clinton Correctional Facility

simply handcuff the inmate to the bed should we need to use the restroom, etc. This was in direct contradiction to all previous departmental training.

One afternoon, while I was assigned to the local hospital, I was tasked with watching an inmate in the Critical Care Unit. He was the brother of a comical, muscle-bound, black inmate who was in Clinton as well. He and I had talked quietly for a short time. The nurse on duty tended to him and moved on to other patients. As the inmate seemed to sleep, it would have been an opportune moment to cuff him to the bed and use the bathroom. Fortunately, I didn't. The inmate began to thrash about the bed and suddenly sat straight up. I asked him if he was OK and he said, "I can't breathe." His eyes rolled back and he fell backward. The alarms to the monitors he was hooked up to never alerted. I called the nurse and she came on the run and immediately coded him. Staff appeared out of nowhere and they shocked him back to life.

Had I taken that short moment to relieve myself, he would have been restrained, alone, and grounded to the bed. It didn't take long for that policy to go out the window after I documented the incident and requested the change in policy in writing from the superintendent. The policy was rescinded and proper security measures were once again implemented.

The Bad Apples

Karma is a wonderful thing and I witnessed many staff members get their dose of it. However, there wasn't always an equal application of justice.

Out of the typical 950 officers and nearly as many civilian staff, there was bound to be a few bad apples in the barrel. I was naive and stubbornly refused to believe that anyone I worked with could possibly be dealing with inmates. That type of stuff only happens in city joints, I believed. That all changed with the arrest of Officer Wally McClure.

Wally was a late-middle-aged, white-haired and bearded yard officer when I arrived at Clinton. He was loud, arrogant and treated junior officers like crap. He bore a striking resemblance to the Travelocity Gnome and always talked about race cars. The last time that he and I worked together was in C-Block on the evening tour. He was covering a swap and I was stuck working with him. Knowing that I swapped a great deal, he tried to get me to swap with him. I kept avoiding the subject. Good thing, too!

One morning, as I was doing my morning workout routine, I had the morning news on the TV. The newscaster led into the story of an arrest being made the night before regarding the introduction of contraband into the prison. "Damn visitors," I muttered. The story continued about the perp being an employee. "Damn civilians," I thought. Then the story revealed that Wally had been receiving money for bringing in alcohol for an inmate. This money was financing his race car! The Inspector General's Office had arranged to have an undercover investigator pose as an inmate's family member and they nabbed him at a restaurant in Plattsburgh. His mug shot showed his arrogance, with his cuffed hands behind his back and a big grin on his face.

One weekend morning I was fortunate enough to work with Mark Young. Mark was a soft-spoken, dry wit, senior officer with an impeccable beard. He knew the jailing business inside and out and he always had some humor to dish out. We were running Lower-F Block 3 and 4 Companies. The weekends are slower and quieter, and things were smooth until a law library runner showed up. These runners pick up and deliver legal materials throughout the facility. As the inmate was delivering on 3 Company, Mark said to me, "We are going to frisk that inmate." 'Sure thing" I replied, and we waited for him to exit the company.

The inmate was ordered to place his hands on the bars of the cage area, the barred walls where the company cell controls are secured within a locked box. He complied and I began to search the items he had in folders as Mark searched his person. Between the two of us, Mark and I recovered over 20 packs of cigarettes. Since cigarettes are used as currency in prison and inmates are only allowed to have two unopened packs on their person at any time, this inmate was looking to chirp.

"Those belong to an officer," he began to repeat over and over again. He revealed who it was and that he was simply collecting and paying off the officer's sporting event bets. Mark was nervous, this was new to see him like this. He stroked his beard over and over as he paced. We simply could not let the inmate walk on this, but we did not want to take an inmate's word against an employee either.

I called the officer to get his reaction and he was clearly nervous. "He's lying!" he yelled and hung up. Mark continued to pace and stroke his beard.

I spoke up, "Let's do it this way. We confiscate the cigarettes, write him up, and keeplock (confined to his cell for 23 hours per day) him. He will go to his hearing and if he sings, he sings. He didn't tell us a damn thing, right? Let them start the investigation." Mark loved the idea and we did exactly that. Mark and I never heard a thing. The officer that the con had fingered transferred to another facility shortly after. Good riddance.

Lisa Gadsen was a short, stout, black female officer working midnights in the Annex. Having transferred from another facility, the rumors abounded. Allegedly, she had been allowed to obliterate the time and attendance rules, which were closely monitored and enforced and still are to this day. She lived in the same town as me and I would often see her waddling about with her gold tooth shining. It wasn't long before she resigned from the department. She had been caught bringing in items for cons. They finally got her fair and square.

There were two very different applications of the rules and regulations within the department: The south of Albany application and the application for the rest of the state. The New York City area was glad to just have enough staff show up to fill their posts. The rest of the state was quick on the draw to issue informal and formal counseling to any employee who might dare have one absence too many in a nine-month period. During my career I witnessed one New York City employee go AWOL for thirteen days, then suddenly return with the biggest line of crap story that he could fabricate and armed with a fraudulent piece of documentation. North of Albany, this same employee would have been fired without discussion. This facility's Staffing Lieutenant didn't care, he was just glad to have an officer back on duty.

One of the greatest examples of the state turning a blind eye to misconduct that I ever witnessed was while I was a lieutenant at a New York City area facility. One member of the administration knew they could trust me and that I handled issues decisively. They once confided in me how relieved other members of the administration were when I was pulling double tours on the weekend, when they wanted peace and quiet.

Even if something occurred, I would handle it, complete any and all paperwork, and then verbally present them with a nicely wrapped package over the phone.

One day, while in one of the administrator's offices, I could see they were frustrated. They had just gotten off the phone with the Inspector General's office. The facility had solid information about a specific female officer engaging in sexual misconduct with an inmate. We knew the who, what, where, why, and how. We also knew who the lookout was – a solid case. The I.G.'s office denied their request for hidden cameras in the area. They pleaded with them, but to no avail. I was brought into the fold.

It does nothing to simply remove a suspected inmate without action against the employee. Once an employee is compromised, they are ripe for further exploitation by the rest of the population. This was a perfect example since she moved on to the next inmate on the list and her activities resumed. She was a willing participant and had no intention of stopping.

"Blaine, you gotta get me transferred. She has her group of inmates searching for the informant. They are getting close to me!" the informant pleaded. The informant was in a panic and I reassured him that he would be safe. He gave me a list of which beds in the dorm were involved and I took it from there. I ordered urinalysis testing on all of the corrupt employee's "posse," as well as a few random inmates from the dorm. Just to muddy the water and confuse them even more, I threw in the informant as well. The only inmate who tested positive for drug use was the inmate the employee was involved with. I nailed him and he went to the Special Housing Unit and she simply moved on to the next inmate. It was clear that she was never going to stop. I am quite certain that it continued after my transfer out.

Power Brokers

During my time as an officer, I witnessed examples of true respect and power. Officer Cliff Brownell and Sergeant Swanson were the employees. Inmates Country and Marks were the examples in green state clothing.

In the 1990s, the administration was harassing Sgt. Swanson and the rank and file were just plain pissed off. Not a soul would ever question his orders, refuse a request, or say a bad word about him. The word went out and the place came to a screeching halt. Nothing moved until the sergeant came to lineup, told us that it was under control, and asked us to return to work. The man had never asked for it to happen - it was respect and the right thing to do.

Cliff Brownell was simply a huge man - big, loud, departmentally as well as politically connected. When his big fist pounded the desk out of frustration, people took notice. I saw this for myself in the administration building when I was being disciplined for allegedly confining an inmate without having filed a misbehavior report, an act that I did not commit. Even the sergeant was bewildered as to why he was ordered by Captain Wilkins to formally counsel me when even the inmate told them that I was not involved!

I sought out Cliff's assistance. He asked me, "Did you do it?"

I replied, "Hell no. Even the inmate told them that I didn't!" That's all it took as we headed upstairs. This was a new experience for me and I was nervous. With me following, he headed to the Deputy Superintendent of Security's office. The voices were a little elevated as Cliff questioned their actions. The DSS began to raise his voice as they argued and it seemed like everyone in the facility could hear it. The captain came on the run and tried to interrupt. Cliff spun around and pointed one of his huge fingers in the captain's face as he yelled, "We aren't talking to you!"

At this point, I felt like I was going to be fired. He turned his attention back to the DSS, who was insisting that the counseling would stand. The DSS also began to yell, accusing me of giving an improper order. Shocked at the lie, I interjected and denied the allegation. I explained what happened. The DSS was clearly confused but started to realize that I was telling the truth. He slowly turned to the now-quiet captain and said, "That isn't what I was told!" The issue was resolved and the targeted "fall guy" was cleared.

I have already detailed inmate Country's influence on the inmate population. I had witnessed respect for many powerful inmates during my career, but inmate Marks was unique. Marks was a tall, thin black man who was housed and worked in the facility hospital. He was incredibly intelligent and was rumored to be one seriously skilled inmate with his fists. He never allowed himself to be on our radar – he was much too smart for that. Marks had respect for staff who did not abuse their authority. It later became apparent that I had his respect.

While I was a sergeant and working my way back to Clinton, I had transferred to another upstate prison in the Clinton hub. On my first day in the block where I was assigned, I made my rounds and addressed issues. As I walked the gallery, suddenly a voice called out from the solid door with the small window, "Blaine, you made it!" I instantly recognized the voice – Marks!

"Those stripes look good on you!" he exclaimed.

"What the hell are you doing here?" I asked him.

He explained that he was becoming a little too popular with the Clinton population. He had received a Misbehavior Report and was being disciplined. He laughed as he said, "I am going to win the appeal but they are going to make me do the time first." Knowing that we were on recorded audio and video, he moved closer to the glass and lowered his voice. "You're not gonna have any problems here," he stated very matter-of-factly.

"No?" I asked.

"No. I'm gonna put the word out," he said. I gave him a wink, a nod, and a smile as I walked away to complete my rounds.

The next morning I began my rounds and it soon became clear that Marks had spoken. Every one of the nearly 240 inmates in that block knew that I was from Clinton, that Marks had worked for me, and that I was a hypnotist. Laughing, I purposely made rounds of his gallery last. He must've gotten a heads up that I was approaching since he was at the door, all smiles. In a low voice, he said, "I put the word out." I told him that I could see that for myself. "You aren't gonna have any problems here. I told these motherfuckers that if they treat you and your people right, they'll have no problems. I also told them that if they get it, they had it coming."

"You didn't lie," I told him and I finished my rounds.

My carpool buddy from the academy later pull me aside and filled me in that the block previously had the reputation as being the hardest to manage. It was supposedly top-heavy with difficult inmates and staff. It was driving the facility's administration crazy that the block that should consume me was running like clockwork. I had a wonderful staff that was working together and getting the job done. Inmate complaints were nearly nonexistent and they even began writing complimentary letters to the superintendent about us. It drove them crazy.

Contraband

Staff are always on the lookout for contraband. It would be impossible to keep track of how many pat frisks one had done throughout their career. Strip frisks, more commonly referred to as "nuts and butts," is one of the least pleasant tasks that an officer will do. It was a close second to one-on-one Special Watches for recovering contraband ingested or secreted within the body cavity. Yes, up their ass.

A Special Watch for contraband is dreaded by everyone. It means that an inmate will be placed in a cell or room, without a toilet or sink. The room is searched before and after each use to be sure that no contraband is present. The officer maintains visual contact at all times and logs the inmate's activity every fifteen minutes. When the inmate needs to defecate, a portable toilet is utilized and the waste is collected. The defecation must be searched for contraband by an officer, typically with a tongue depressor.

Inmates are creative and sly. We always tried to catch up to their latest methods and new contraband during my later years, such as the flood of synthetic marijuana known as K2 and the synthetic drug Suboxone as well. However, the routine search for the usual drugs, gang materials, weapons, etc., kept us busy. Most supervisors appreciated the keen eye of their staff. Some did not.

Lieutenant Harding was an example of the latter. He was a loud, mean-mouthed, lazy, arrogant man who belittled everyone. He despised anyone who made him get out of his chair and do something. My buddy, Danny, was a vigilant housing unit officer and was constantly finding contraband in the housing unit common areas. These are areas such as the shower, restroom, kitchen, behind radiators and in the TV room. The inmates would file complaints about him and each one had to be investigated. This meant that the lieutenant had to assign it to the area supervisor to conduct the investigation and obtain the officer's written statement. When Danny discovered that the window bars in the shower area had cut marks, he searched the area and recovered a hacksaw blade from the sink drain. This officer's diligence and actions should have been acknowledged and commended, but that simply was not this watch commander's way of doing business. Lt. Harding accused him of bringing the contraband in and threatened to "get him." Danny refused to ever exercise that level of vigilance again. A good officer was embittered and it affects the rest of the staff. Later in my career, in that same exact watch commander capacity, I would utilize any extra staff to actively search for contraband and enjoyed a very high recovery rate. It showed that we were doing our jobs.

One of the most memorable contraband items I recovered was a butter box cut out and colored black to look like a pistol in lower light conditions. It had been secreted in the hospital porters' dorm kitchen. Within an hour of us removing all of the extra privileges they received, an inmate stepped forward and claimed ownership. The others had pushed him to do it. He had no choice. They were not willing to take the heat for his stupidity.

It takes a lot to impress me, but one con did. Most inmates are busy making weapons or secreting drugs, but not this guy. He was an entrepreneur. I had been sent to search his cell but was not given any clue as to what they were seeking. I looked and looked and was puzzled, then I discovered it – a pyramid scheme! It was brilliant and I read the pages of mailing lists, the copies of letters and instructions. This guy was realizing a small, steady income, and felt like he was not doing anything wrong. I think he finally figured out how wrong he was at his disciplinary hearing.

One of the best pieces of equipment was the BOSS chair. It would scan the body cavity of the individual sitting in it for metal. The Body Orifice Security Scanner was more commonly referred to as the "Ass Master 5000" or countless other slang terms, but it was very effective.

The public is bewildered as to how contraband is introduced into prisons. The number one source is the visits that inmates receive. Visiting rooms are a zoo, and it only takes a split-second to swallow a balloon of drugs that a visitor smuggled in. The old prison movies that show thick glass separating the inmates from their visitors do not exist. For an inmate to warrant non-contact visits, it seemingly takes an act of Congress.

Tiers of Laughter

The last place you would expect to be entertained or hear howling laughter would be in a maximum-security prison, but the opposite is true. People do the darnedest things and staff with idle time would, in record time, draw and circulate cartoons of each other's antics. Nobody was safe from the skills of a jailhouse artist. Past events never simply died but were brought up over and over again. Many are re-lived yet again when retirees gather and share a drink.

Officer Brian Dabney and I were longtime friends and had each other's backs in this often vicious environment. Brian was a loyal, jovial, intelligent man with a heart of gold, but there was something that set him apart from everyone there: his unmistakable voice. Brian had suffered an injury years earlier and it had affected his voice. Many people had difficulty understanding him, but I, for some reason, had none. Worse yet, I could imitate him perfectly. Whenever I answered for him in lineup or called someone, posing as him, it always had someone calling Brian and chewing him out for something he didn't do.

One evening I called a buddy named Pete who worked in a housing unit as I posed as Brian. He asked why I was still on duty since Brian was a day shift officer. I lied and explained that I was unexpectedly forced to work overtime on a housing unit and had no dinner. Pete, having a soft spot for people in a jam, offered to send over half of his dinner – a sausage sandwich. I accepted, hung up and called the real housing officer and told him that a sandwich was on its way and to enjoy it with no questions asked. The officer was surprised and readily accepted it. Within a few hours, Pete realized that he had been had.

One weekend, while I was still an officer and assisting in the Special Housing Unit, I reached out to Brian, who was working in A-Block. He was talking a mile a minute, trying to get off the phone and get over to D-Block where breakfast was waiting for him. I tried to playfully delay him, but Brian hung up on me. Hang up on me? Ok, the game was on. I called D-Block, posing as Brian and asked if they had more food available for the other officers in A-Block. The officer said no and that if I didn't get over there fast, they would give it away. Little did they know that Brian was actually about three minutes from the block. I began to yell into the phone, "To hell with it then, give it away. If you don't have enough for everyone, I don't want it!" Then I slammed down the phone. The officer gave away the plate of food and Brian showed up just after that. He was a little more than steamed at me when the D-Block officer explained that he had received a call from him, yelling at him for not having more. He returned to A-Block empty-handed.

The queen mother of all impersonations occurred while I was working in the Annex, covering the shift of a friend who had recently covered for me. Part of my assignment for the day was to pick up the count slips from all over the facility and deliver them to the watch commander. As I hurriedly passed through one housing unit to another, I arrived at Brian's unit. Knowing that the watch commander that day, Lieutenant Richardson, was on duty, it was a perfect scenario to play with him. I asked Brian if he wanted to have some fun. He was typically on the receiving end of the fun so he quickly said, "Yeah!" I told him to just go along with what I said and I went to work. I called the lieutenant, posing as Brian. He answered in his standard "Lieutenant Richardson," and I went about telling him that I had brought a cell phone into the facility and I was going to call him back in a few minutes to see what kind of signal I could get from inside. Bringing a cell phone into prison back then was grounds for instant termination. The lieutenant began to go nuts, sternly saying that I had better not have brought a phone in. I insisted that I had and I told him that I would call him back. I hung up on him and Brian and I broke into laughter. We could hardly breathe as we replayed it over and over. I swore Brian to not reveal that it was me and away I went to collect the other counts. When I arrived in the clinic area, I used their outside line to call the main facility phone number. I entered the watch commander extension and waited. Lieutenant Richardson, hearing the double ring of an outside call, sprang to life and, in his most professional voice, answered the phone. In my best Brian impersonation, I explained that I was calling from my cell phone while on the housing unit and I simply could not believe the clarity and quality of the call. He began to yell into the phone and I could hear him pounding the desk with his fist. Right in the middle of his tirade, I said, "Can you hear me now?" and I hung up. The man was livid!

The lieutenant sent up a freshly transferred sergeant to search Brian's work area and property for the cell phone. He asked Brian about the call and Brian laughed as he explained that it had been me all along. The sergeant was well aware of my spot-on impersonation and simply shook his head and said, "Blaine, that explains everything." Then he walked away.

There were countless other instances where I impersonated my buddy. I would volunteer him for assignments, or simply toy with people, but it was never done to ridicule him. We were, and still are, friends to this day. I have a great amount of respect for this man who overcame so many obstacles in life and lived to reap the rewards.

Nothing is better than when the jokester is the victim. In this case, it was the most senior officer in the facility being forgotten at a rest area on the interstate while transporting inmates on the draft bus. Jim Drake was a tall farmer and was always messing with people. His bid job was on the draft bus, which transported inmates being transferred throughout the state. One day a sergeant with a head that largely resembled a pumpkin was assigned to the bus. They stopped at a rest area and each staff member took a turn using the facilities. Jim was the last to go. He exited from the special rear, caged area, security door and went in. When he finally emerged, the bus was gone! Jim initially thought that he was the butt of a joke, but within seconds panic set in. He utilized the departmental cell phone in his possession and called 911. He explained the situation and a state trooper arrived very shortly after. They raced down the interstate. Jim then ambled up on the bus, took his place, and the trip resumed.

As the story was laid out for me by Jim, the inmates onboard tried to alert the sergeant that he had forgotten someone. Not wanting to hear anything from a convict nor see what the excitement was about, he'd ordered them to shut up and he gave the driver the command to go. The cons complied and the driver did as he was told. When I learned of this I had visions of Jim emerging from the bathroom with his pants around his ankles and toilet paper trailing behind him in a resemblance to the actor Steve Martin in the movie, *The Jerk.* Though a dangerous situation, envisioning Jim left behind still makes me laugh to this day. And the sergeant in charge? Well, nobody can figure out how he survived that one with his chevrons intact, so one can only assume that his close association with the superintendent saved his ass.

Throughout the state, there are countless tales of humor behind the walls and fences of correctional facilities. Corrections employees see humor in what others on the streets find disgusting, offensive, or revolting. This is probably one of the clearest examples of the effects on the staff working in the system.

Clinton Has a Hypnotist

My two jobs could not be any more different, yet they provided the balance I needed to make it all work. New York State can be inconsistent and fickle, so I had no idea how they would react to my being a hypnotist. The time had come when I could no longer hide my bustling outside career and upcoming public show announcements. The Employee Manual rules require obtaining permission for outside employment. I submitted mine and waited, and waited, and waited. It wasn't until I was upstairs in the administration building when I asked Superintendent Simmons if there were any issues with my application. I told him that I realized it was unusual, but it had been many months since I had submitted it. He did not recall it and asked me, "What do you do?"

With a smile, I replied, "I'm a hypnotist."

I have never seen such an unintentionally comedic response as this man, the superintendent of the largest prison in New York State, suddenly became very interested in his shoes. He shot questions at me with only split-second glances as he asked each one: "Where did you learn that? Any good at it?" I could barely contain my laughter until I got out of the office.

The superintendent was a bit nervous around me so I just had to use it to my advantage. As he would make rounds I would utilize my Neuro-Linguistic Programming (NLP) skills that I had been taught while being certified in hypnotherapy. As Mr. Simmons approached, I would extend my hand, he would grasp it, and I would smile until he nervously pulled his hand away. Over the years it became a game and I won every time.

He was fascinated that I was performing all over the USA. He often asked

Author's publicity photo from the late 1990s

how I promoted myself, etc. Just before he retired, I suckered him into the handshake one last time. This time I held on longer than ever as he repeatedly tried to pull away. He was nervously laughing as he grabbed the hospital's medication room window bars and used it to pull himself away. All this time, the captain accompanying him was visibly nervous as he shook his head in disbelief, clearly hoping that he was not seeing what was happening before him.

The Training Academy Christmas party coordinator had asked if I would perform for their event in Albany and I gladly accepted. When I was approximately a third of the way through my show with one of the Special Ops members, Fernando was curled up and incredibly deep in a trance on the floor. I looked up and noticed that the commissioner had arrived and was watching as he was talking on his phone. I thought little of it until Fernando's pager sounded. The commissioner, not believing what he was seeing, had the Command Center activate the pager! When his guy didn't spring to life, he realized that what he was witnessing was very, very real!

I just snicker when I am asked, "Did you ever hypnotize an inmate?" I can say that I repeatedly used my acquired skills to diffuse many dangerous situations where hostile, dangerous inmates were unknowingly and slowly brought down to a manageable state with no hypnosis utilized. More than once an extremely agitated, handcuffed inmate would be brought to the Mental Health area for examination and admission to one of the OBS areas. Staff would jokingly suggest that I hypnotize them as I sat on a bench opposite the inmate. I would begin the conversation at the inmate's tone and volume and slowly bring it down. Once I had the desired level, I would simply describe how well the staff would take care of them and to consider it as a few days of vacation. Without fail, the inmate would not only be interviewed and admitted without incident, and they would be sound asleep after having their evening meal. Kids' stuff.

Being a comedy stage hypnotist in a prison provided some humorous times as well. The funniest was on a rare occasion when two of the day shift officers were working swaps with me in the prison hospital.

Roger and Donny were nonstop jokesters and no prank was off-limits, especially on each other. Roger was relentless in insisting that I hypnotize Donny that evening. My prospective hypnotic subject kept insisting that he would cooperate with my directions. I told Roger that there was no way that this would work with him standing there, watching and salivating in anticipation. He headed back to the first floor where he was assigned but made me swear that I would call for him when Donny was entranced. I agreed and away he went.

"OK, Donny," I told him. "We both know that you are never going to let me work with you, so let's have some fun with Roger." Donny's face lit up and he was all ears. "Just go along with everything I say," I explained. "You just pretend to be hypnotized and we will get his ass good." I never thought he could do it with a straight face, but the guy gave a performance that was worthy of an Academy Award.

We chose one of the prison's old exam rooms, complete with an operating table. Having seated him in a comfortable chair, I wheeled one alongside for myself. The stage was set and we were ready to roll. I had the nurse call Roger and tell him that Donny was hypnotized. I knew he'd come on the run – and he did. Roger was a big man and we heard his feet on the upper stairs and his key work the lock. He breathed heavily as he made his way into the room and I quietly told him to stand directly in front of his "hypnotized" buddy. It was showtime.

"Donny," I said, "When I count to three, you will open your eyes. You will see in front of you the most beautiful woman in the world. She's hot and she's horny but she wants you as much as you want her. She may resist a little but she likes it that way!" As I started my count to three, I could see Roger about to burst out with laughter. "1… 2… 3… open your eyes and there she is!" I said and Donny flew out of his chair. He began to fondle, feel and kiss his new "girlfriend" who was laughing, crying, and trying to ward off his attacker. It didn't take Donny very long to overpower his victim. In short order, he had Roger bent over the operating table, dry humping and trying to kiss him. Roger was begging me to make him stop.

I gave Donny the command to stop and to return to his chair. I ordered him to return to sleep and Roger disappeared. We heard the door close and then together we burst out laughing, swearing secrecy to each other. We both wondered if we should call the Rape Crisis Hotline for Roger. We did what so few people ever accomplished, we got one over on this very shrewd man!

Within a week of the escape of the two inmates, I had already developed and started the process of trademarking the phrase, "You Cannot Escape My Trance". I continue using it to this day.

Changes in the Administration

Doug Ambler was rumored to be promoted from Special Ops to First Deputy Superintendent at Clinton. I had been introduced to him through my cousin, Brian Jenkins, a fellow Special Ops employee in Albany. We had hit it off and enjoyed communicating with one another. He had risen to the top quickly in his career and I admired his ability. It was no secret that if the right people took a liking to you that your career path would be laid out before you with few bumps to avoid. He was one of them. His goals were power and speeding through one promotion as fast as he could to get to the next. We had little in common but he admired my drive and talents. I was self-made and that was something he could never claim.

"Special Ops, Jenkins," Brian said as he answered his phone. I filled him in on the latest rumor at Clinton, that Doug was being promoted here.

"Oh yeah?" he said. I heard him call around the corner to Doug's office, "Doug, the latest rumor at Clinton is that you are being promoted to First Dep there." I could hear Doug shout back, "Tell Blaine to stop spreading rumors!" It was laughable since Brian had never told him who was on the line.

In less than two months, it happened just as the rumors had said it would. Doug reported to Clinton. He later told me that he truly had no clue about the promotion rumor and was amazed that we knew about it first. The writing was on the wall that our current superintendent, Donald Simmons, was to retire and Doug was being groomed to be his replacement. Doug was youthful and full of energy as he dove into his work. He was personable and people felt at ease talking to him, not like past First Deputy Superintendents. He had risen through the security ranks at an early age. These young, fast track supervisors were commonly referred to as the "Whiz Kids."

I had warned Doug before he even reported to the facility as the First Deputy Superintendent at Clinton: "Clinton is a big, clunking machine. Each day it just clunks on and on. It takes very little maintenance; just a little oil here and there keeps it running. If it ever shuts down on you, there is a reason and there is nothing you can do to start it up again until you fix the problem. That is all I am going to tell you." The voice on the other end of the line was trying to digest what I was saying. They clearly didn't listen.

I was a bit nervous about being friends with an administrator and this was all new to me. People would be suspicious and accusatory if they knew that he had been to my home, our kids played together, and I knew about his failing marriage. He was very upset about his wife having an affair with a priest, and he hid it well. I soon learned that he was a coward, just a puppet in a suit who would dance to any tune Albany played. I would be the first employee in Clinton he would screw over as superintendent. We would soon become mortal enemies. I hate him to this very day. Survival and self-preservation would soon become very necessary.

Survival

Doug had been promoted to superintendent at Clinton upon the retirement of Mr. Simmons. The facility was a little more jovial and relaxed. We had a youthful, security-minded leader who interacted with us more. My wife, Helen, had left her position as a secretary in the Mental Health Unit for a clean, warm office as a clerk at SUNY Plattsburgh. Little did I know that she had been maintaining a lesbian relationship with a social worker, Betty, from the prison. Betty was a scrawny, ugly woman who was scared of her own shadow. With an alcoholic past, she was a train wreck who had been pushed out of her most recent relationship. Her lesbian partner had teamed up with their hairdresser - you just couldn't make this crap up.

Helen dropped that bomb on me as I was out of town for four days of performing. Over the phone, she said that she wanted a divorce so she could be with a woman, Betty. It was obvious that she had already met with an attorney. I had been blindsided, and now I would soon learn that weapons come in all shapes, sizes, genders, and sexualities.

Before heading to Massachusetts earlier that day, I had stopped by Helen's job. Something had been bothering her and she was on edge. It was bad enough living with her mother while the new house was being built. I hated her family and the way they raised their children in the same cold and financially irresponsible way in which they'd been raised. They were rude, thieving and untrustworthy. Not a single one of my wife's siblings could support themselves. Every one of them seemed to believe that they would hit the lottery and live happily ever after. They resented me for my success and I despised them for their sloth.

It was going to be impossible to return to work at the prison Tuesday. If that bitch, Betty or anyone else taunted me or gloated, it simply would not end well. I needed to step away and regroup. Calling in sick was my only option. I called the facility Chart Sergeant and called in sick until further notice without giving any details. No one yet knew, but there was no way it would stay like that for very long.

I returned to work after a few days and I was fulfilling my swap obligations. I dreaded putting on my uniform and my heart raced faster and faster as I neared the dungeon. I settled into my post for the day tour in the dental office. Needing to leave the area for an escort, I was met by Kevin Favor, a civilian who thrived on ridiculing others. He was a scumbag of the very worst sort. He sat at a desk in the mental health unit and read novels for years with no real job to perform. I despised him. As I descended the stairs, I suspected he was going to put some salt on my wound as he turned to me and with his smiling, fat, rat face said, "Hi, Mike."

I leaned to within a few inches of his face and looked deep into his black soul and told him in the coldest voice I could muster, "Fuck you." The look on his face was a true sight to behold. He was scared shitless and he went his way. He simply wasn't man enough to address it. I later found out that he'd had no idea about my situation and went to his work station, crying. It seems that I had, with a few words, ruined all of the therapy he had been receiving. That first day back was the longest I have ever experienced in my career.

Work was going well. I realized that relatively few people knew, or were respectfully keeping it quiet. I never saw the home-wrecking bitch until one day as I walked from the parking lot to the front gate. I was walking with an RN who worked in close proximity to my job. We suddenly saw Betty emerge from the front gate and head up the walkway, directly for us. As she passed by I stopped in my tracks and just looked and felt pleasure as she refused to look me in the eye. A week later, while walking in the hall with a fellow officer, I again encountered the dyke and she purposefully and intentionally made a beeline for us. It was necessary for us to quickly split, to allow her to pass without being struck despite the left side of the hall being open and clear. Betty then stopped in her tracks, and in her bitchy, nervous tone called out, "Oh yeah? I'll fix you!" then she stormed off.

My friend, Steve asked me, "What was that about?" I was shocked to learn that he had no idea of my separation. He indicated that it all made sense now.

Self-Preservation

Doug had told me that Betty had been filing allegations of harassment. I asked him what they were and he said it had something to do with the parking lot and a hallway. I told him that I had witnesses to both encounters but he didn't want to discuss it. I asked him for an investigation and he refused. I told him that allegations of employee misconduct must be investigated and he stated that they simply were not going to address them. He directed me to see the Deputy Superintendent for Security, DSS Thomas. I warned him that without an investigation and her being called on the carpet, she would only make more allegations and that I would not always have a witness. Again he refused. "Let the chips fall where they may," I said to him as we parted. The friendship was over.

As directed, I met with former Captain, now DSS Thomas. He confirmed the existence of the allegations I was refused the ability to read, respond, or present eyewitnesses. I asked him to conduct an investigation that would undoubtedly clear me and again I was denied. I explained that my soon-to-be-ex and I were communicating, and as long as I played ball and was a good boy I was to get the settlement of a lifetime, to no avail. It was clear that Betty's sexuality and gender would be given preferential consideration, so I asked what they expected me to do and he said, "Mike, we suggest you go work in the Annex for a while."

I refused to give up my job bidding and seniority rights and stood my ground. "You want me to run and hide?" I asked.

"No," he said. "Mike, we do not consider it running and hiding. We consider it survival and self-preservation."

I immediately went out on leave. There was no way I could risk losing my job right now.

I called my cousin, Brian, who was now a Deputy Superintendent at another facility and asked him for a favor. After explaining the false accusations and my fear of being set up, I asked him to take possession of all my personal firearms. He told me to get them over there as soon as I could and within 45 minutes he had them all. He left me with his familiar advice once more: "Keep making good decisions."

Betty did just as I had predicted. Not getting satisfaction, she increased her attacks by making allegations every time she saw me. Her new attack was alleging that I'd made a verbal threat to kill her. As a result, I was questioned at length by a butch female state police trooper who had come into the interview with predetermined conclusions, as she had prepared the official charge beforehand. She then issued a charge and I had to face a judge. Refusing to accept any plea and seeing through her threats, we were soon headed to trial.

January 6, 2004's mail brought me a certified letter from my superintendent. I was suspended, or more commonly referred to as being "locked out" until I was seen and cleared to return to duty by a New York state psychiatrist in Albany. They refer to it as an Employee Health Services physical. How much more salt could they throw on my wound? Hadn't they hurt me enough? I was numb from their stupidity and miscalculated actions. The administration at Clinton continued to cover up their mistakes by trying to paint me as the problem in the equation.

Finally, later in January 2004, I was interviewed by an investigator for the New York state insurance fund. The gentleman, named Roger Steele, was an employee for a private agency contracted by the state. Mr. Steele was decent, yet utilized a hostile, accusatory tone with me at first.

I walked him through the incident that forced me to leave my job and the chain of events that followed. By the time I was done this guy's jaw was nearly hitting the table and he had no way of hiding his shock.

"Let me get this straight," he said. "They would not let you read the complaints, respond to them, or present eyewitnesses that would clear you?"

"Yes," I said.

"No wonder you flipped!" he shot at me. I couldn't believe that someone was finally seeing what I was going through and was putting it all on paper.

My next interview was with the Inspector General's Office. Investigator Richard Allen was even more cordial and decent as he seemed to extend to me every courtesy possible. His decency had me suspecting a setup, so I proceeded with caution as I answered his questions. Just as in the state insurance fund interview, the investigator's jaw dropped and was completely floored when he learned that I was accused and was suggested to relocate without any response from me or my witnesses being interviewed. He assured me that starting that very afternoon each of my eyewitnesses would be interviewed. I thanked the guy and shook his hand. One of the documents that helped clear me was Betty's timesheet. She had accused me of misconduct in the parking lot at 2:20 pm but had signed out, indicating that she had ended her workday at 3:00 pm. She was going to be forced to pick which lie to pursue. These I.G. guys are usually trying to fire us and this guy seemed to see the truth: The facility administration was wrong in what they'd done to me and they were trying to bury it, and me, with it. Quite some time later, it was confidentially disclosed to me that Betty was told to drop the phony charges or face disciplinary and possible legal action for lying and falsifying state documents. An arrest would also jeopardize her professional license.

The day of my Employee Health Services examination had arrived. Dressed in a suit and tie, typical business professional attire, I was a bit early for the appointment but had a minimal wait as I was greeted by Dr. Andrews. He escorted me to his office and I could feel him sizing me up. I had my defenses up and was fully prepared to do battle. He introduced himself, explained in detail that he was a psychiatrist but only worked part-time for the state. He told me that he did this to supplement his own practice and that he didn't receive any sick or vacation time, so he didn't have any real loyalty to the state. As he said this he leaned and stared at me, starting to take on a bolder, more aggressive tone as he now pointed a finger at me and boomed, "I'm here for one thing and one thing only. Do I send you back to work or not?"

"Doc," I replied, "I never wanted to leave my job. My being out of work is costing me a fortune." The doctor was visibly confused. He rifled through the file on me and asked how it was financially affecting me since I was suspended using my accruals. I explained to the man that I was self-employed and I should have had my time off for summer performing nearly all lined up. Being out of work would not allow me to have my time off lined up for the summer tour.

Dr. Andrews was amazed at my side occupation and then asked me about the situation at the facility. I explained everything in detail and as I did I spied a document in the folder on the table. I read it – upside down – and nearly fell off my chair. The document was the single piece of paper that had gotten me suspended. In short, it detailed how my estranged spouse worked in close proximity to my post. It continued to say that I had called the facility, spoke to a supervisor, and stated that if I should see her in the hallway and with the least provocation, even a wink, I would most likely assault her.

"Doctor, is this the thing that got me locked out?" I demanded as I kept hitting the file with my finger.

"Yes," he replied.

I took control of the interview now and continued to demand answers. My heart was racing and again I hopped up and down in my chair, unable to compose myself. "Doctor, don't you people check the validity of a statement before you lock someone out?" I demanded.

"No, why?" he asked.

"Call Clinton right now and speak to anyone with any time there. They will tell you that this statement is false!" I challenged. He now demanded to know what I meant.

"Doctor," I explained, "my ex hasn't worked there for 3 ½ years!"

The doctor fell back in his chair and let out a long, long breath and nervously began to run his fingers through his hair. I had discovered the smoking gun and I begged the doctor to cite the error in his report. He informed me that he needed to consult with his boss and returned to me shortly after. "Yes, I can do it," he said.

At the end of the interview, Dr. Andrews insisted that I file the necessary paperwork at the front desk to obtain a copy of his report. He recognized that several errors had been made and he took me by the wrist to the desk and he watched me fill out the document. He wished me well as we said goodbye and shook hands. In his report, he indicated that I should be commended for my mental state for what I had been through. I felt like a million bucks. People were starting to realize the truth.

Finally, the afternoon for my trial had arrived. I was representing myself and had subpoenaed IG Investigator Allen to testify on my behalf. Court was late and he walked into the room, approached me and asked me why I had summoned him to appear. "I am going to ask you one question and one question only," I explained. "Can you say that in good faith that during your investigation that the complainant has a history of lying and falsifying state documents?"

He looked directly at me and said, "Yes."

The butch female trooper entered from the back of the room with an angry look on her face as the judge entered from the front. "People versus Michael Blaine!" he bellowed. "Michael Blaine, approach the bench." I approached and was prepared to argue. The judge looked at the trooper and asked, "Trooper, do you have a motion to make?"

"Motion to dismiss, Your Honor. She called today and wants the charges dropped." The trooper was pissed that she'd had her time wasted and there was no fruit to pick within the complaint.

My jaw dropped as I turned around and looked at the IG investigator. He was as shocked as I was. We walked out together and he confided in me that after we had initially met, he had gone home to his wife and said, "If you ever leave me, please don't do me the way they did this guy." He had never seen an officer screwed over worse.

Here We Go Again

I was ordered back to duty and away I went. I was anticipating my promotion to sergeant and sought a change until it happened. I submitted several job bids. Open positions are awarded by seniority and, miraculously, I was awarded the sweetest shift at the facility - 6:00 am-2:00 pm.

I quickly learned to appreciate this new tour of duty. The shift was in before the place came to life and we were out before it came down from its hustle and bustle. The 2:00 pm-10:00 pm shift had a tough time finding guys to swap with on my tour and they lined up to work with me. Only one problem and I didn't care, increased contact with Betty. She had given it her best shot and failed miserably. The administration did nothing to rein her in and it soon set the facility abuzz.

While assigned to fill in another officer's two-week vacation slot, I was assigned to the Visiting Room Gate in the main. I was engaged in a lighthearted conversation with Officer Tanya Bennett and Lt. George Ryan when Betty and Marge, Betty's hefty, former lesbian partner, approached my area. I swung open the large, heavy steel gate, stepped back and looked forward. As she passed by, Betty felt it necessary to mark her ground. She walked up to me, steered toward me, leaned in my direction and struck her shoulder into my chest as she passed by. I didn't move and I did not engage. I was a statue.

I closed and secured the gate by flipping the large key in the cylinder and asked my witnesses, "How much more do I have to take?"

Tanya was livid. "Hasn't she done enough? She is trying to get you to do something!" Lt. Ryan was a company man and did nothing. His uselessness would be demonstrated to an even higher degree in future years. I learned shortly after that his first wife had left him for a woman as well.

I documented the incident and sent it to the office of the Superintendent. Ambler. It was clear that no action would be taken. No agency or department would address the issue. "She is a protected class of person," I was informed. She knew how to play the system. It wasn't until after I wrote the governor's office that the issue was finally investigated. Six months later, I finally - after demanding the results - learned that their finding concluded that the incident did occur, but there was no malfeasance since I did not appear to be upset nor did I voice an objection. My written response to them was clear and to the point as I informed them that if she touches me again I would use any force necessary to defend myself. I would never be a victim again. They never responded.

The rest of my days as an officer were tense. I filed many grievances on the mistreatment that I was forced to endure. One day, while assigned to the Lower F Corridor Gate, I saw Superintendent Ambler approach. He entered my area and we were alone. I locked us in between the gates and pointed the key right at him. I towered above him and there was no respect in my voice whatsoever. "This is getting out of hand. People think they are helping you. I warned you, now I am telling you. Tell your people to keep out of this." He asked what had happened and I refused to give examples. I gave him enough to chew on and his eye indexing cues and body language screamed that he was digesting the information. Mission accomplished.

Chevrons and Payback

I received the call and was offered three choices for a sergeant's post – all in the New York City area. I chose Staten Island and away I went. It was a very unusual place. The Deputy Superintendent for Security there was a very decent, hard-working black man who hated corruption. We soon had a great working relationship. However, with each promotion comes a probationary period of one year. Some less-than-ethical administrators like to take advantage of this and exact revenge.

My first day as the Housing Sergeant resulted in a five-man fight with three uses of force. Just another day for me, but it was chaos for this facility. I gathered the staff and set them to writing, thinking that they were as experienced as me – wrong! As I looked over their shoulders, I was shocked at what they were writing. I ordered them to all stop and gave them a lesson in Report Writing. They were apprehensive until I explained that I was from Clinton and we had perfected this process. We knocked it out in record time.

I could not understand why I kept getting all types of assignments that the other sergeants didn't and it was revealed later on that it was the DSS's doing. He liked the work that I produced and the judgment I used. He had already asked me to withdraw my transfer and I had. The second time I submitted one he told me that he understood but asked me why. "Sir, we both know that I did not come down here in Clinton's good graces," I started.

He was mulling over what I had said. "No, I wasn't aware, but that explains the phone calls I have been getting, checking up on you." He never disclosed who had called, but he did explain that he informed the callers that he had hoped that I would stay and wished that he had more like me.

Just a few months after being promoted, I received news about Clinton. The staff had had enough of Superintendent Ambler's antics and decided to take matters into their own hands. I wondered why it had taken so long for it to finally happen. The staff decided to run the facility according to their job descriptions. Ambler made it worse by laughing at the staff, saying that the afternoon shift would come in and it would run normally. The facility may have been running slow, but now the machine had stopped. He had ignored my advice about how Clinton works. He had nobody to blame but himself. I would have given anything to have been there. The smile on my face as he passed by would have infuriated him.

On about the fifth day, he went to lineup. He pleaded with the staff to get the place on track and running again. Officers present said that he was clearly a beaten man whose voice was shaky and nervous. He had been humbled and was now bestowed with the unofficial "Longest Slowdown" titleholder. It was a title without honor or glory. The whiz kid had screwed up and had to own it. The machine was fixed, but the damage was done. The young staff had been empowered. They were taking for granted the power that the old-time union men had earned. The superintendent was now afraid to create waves. He had created monsters who felt that they could do as they wish. I would soon see this in the younger staff upon my return.

As soon as I transferred back to the Clinton hub – the group of facilities within the Clinton region – the retaliation resumed. Despite outperforming my probationary peers and most of the seasoned supervisors, I was given substance ratings on my evaluations. This would continue on and on and my evaluators were nervous. After all, they were simply following the direction they were being given. They were hungry for promotions and afraid of being targeted in the same manner that I was subjected to. I just shook my head and focused on the job.

One supervisor, a short, squat, administrative sycophant, worked on me for over 20 minutes, trying to piss me off one night. Alone in the office with him, I kept laughing at his tactics, then he crossed a line. I felt rage build up and I knew that I had to get out of the room or it would become physical. He ordered me to sit down and I questioned his actions. He barked at me again and I snapped. About six seconds after he gave that last order, he suddenly realized that he was no longer in control of that discussion. He was scared shitless, having just seen a side of me that very few had. He could barely pull himself together enough to order me out of the room. It all came to an end months later when I'd finally had enough.

Someone had finally listened. They looked into the nonstop harassment and mishandling of my complaints. It all stopped right there and then - for now. David Giguere was one particularly nasty, egotistical little man who was allegedly forced into a promotion that he had repeatedly turned down since it was a promotion in title only and farther away. I was finally allowed to do my job and be judged on my merits. This, in conjunction with an arbitration settlement guaranteeing me a review of any issues by the arbitrator, smoothed the road.

I returned to Clinton with a smile on my face that clearly pissed off Superintendent Ambler. Although it had been nearly a year and a half since the staff had spanked him, he was still a very humbled man. Betty, the social worker, and my ex had relocated. Happy days were here again. Or were they? There were a few issues between Ambler and me, but he was aware that people were watching. Every Use of Force I had was being scrutinized and he desperately looked for something, anything, to get me. To no avail.

In 2007, Annex Captain Griese – a complete slob – was overhead by an officer saying, "I never want to be at the receiving end of Blaine's pen." He was also heard saying, "Well, Blaine pulled a rabbit out of his hat again!" after I had been cleared of any misconduct after a Use of Force interview with the IG. Superintendent. Ambler thought he smelled an opportunity to utilize them to get at me. He failed.

I was a union steward at this point and Ambler wasn't happy about it. When he was in a labor-management meeting and made a statement regarding two officer's mental state, I blew a gasket. I stopped the meeting and reminded him that nobody in the room, including him, was qualified to make an assessment. He was caught and he stared at his shoes as his face became beet red. He conceded and we moved on to the next topic. My fellow union reps congratulated me for achieving what no one else could. It became the talk of the facility.

Unexpected Reunions

As time passed on and the days flew by, the ocean of inmates dressed in state-issued green clothing rolled in and out like the tide. The nonstop transfers from one facility to another meant that they may have gone away, but that did not mean that our paths would not cross again, either in or out of prison.

One of the most memorable reunions I remember, while still on the job, was on my very first day as a lieutenant, May 19, 2008. I had accepted the promotion on Staten Island, where I had previously been promoted to Sergeant 3 1/2 years earlier. I accompanied the watch commander that day, the resident lying sack of incompetent crap, Freddy the Fibber. Freddy had earned his nickname because every time his lips moved lies came out. His incompetence created an extra workload for me as I was tasked with cleaning up his messes all of the time. Within eleven months, Freddy the Fibber would accuse me of beating the crap out of him while on duty. I do admit that the thought did cross my mind more than just a few times, but his cowardice saved his dumb ass.

As we passed through the housing units and I met newer staff and reunited with old friends, I caught a glimpse of a familiar face, that of an inmate. Our eyes met and the inmate immediately looked away and downward, trying to escape my notice, but it was too late! It may have been nearly 20 years since we'd known each other, and there was gray in his hair, but the face was the same. My memory raced back to Green Haven in the fall of 1988. In E-Block, he'd been a young porter who always tried to scam and get something over on new officers. I never gave him an inch and we butted heads daily. The most memorable event occurred when someone had left his cell and the slop sink open. I'd arrived and ordered him out of the slop sink. He kept trying to delay me and I gave a final order and he stuck his head out. I couldn't stop laughing as this man emerged, covered with soap. Since cells do not have hot water, he was taking a "bird bath." I took the opportunity to teach him a lesson about getting over on newer staff. He pouted and shuffled back to his cell, covered in soap to finish his rinse in cold water from his sink.

I chuckled to myself at his shock in recognizing me. I walked up to him and said, "We are both a little older and a whole lot smarter, aren't we?" He couldn't even speak, he just nodded repeatedly and smiled, obviously relieved. Within a few days, I saw him again and we laughed about those days. He could not believe that I instantly recognized him and he told me that my look hadn't changed in all those years. He told me that jail had been tough on him and the new inmates lacked respect for others and themselves as well.

Other reunions unexpectedly took place outside of the walls of Dannemora. As a performer, I never knew who was watching my show. The fall of 2014, just after my retirement, proved my point. I was performing at a fair just outside of Albany and had given the crowd a great show. I quickly packed up my props and cleared the stage for the next show. Several audience members had gathered near the stage, wanting to meet me. I answered their questions and thanked them for their compliments, but one person hung back and waited for the others to leave. Then he inquired about hypnosis to assist his wife in her battle to stop smoking. The conversation continued and I knew that there was something familiar about this man. We had met before, but I simply could not place him. I told him that we had met and asked what he did for a living. He asked me if I had been a correction officer and I replied that I had recently retired as a lieutenant. He asked if I had worked at Clinton and again I stated that I had. His statement, "Well, I did 17 years there," floored me and I suddenly realized who it was. "Victor Hicks, you son-of-a-bitch!"

Victor was well-known at Clinton. He was a very talented artist who had painted murals in the mess halls and some other units where his skills could be utilized. When the state had hobby shops at each facility, the staff could legitimately order and purchase arts and crafts from the inmates. Few people knew that Victor had developed his artistic skills under the teaching of my cousin, Brian, when he was a civilian instructor there before becoming an officer. Victor's brothers had done time as well and were equally talented. I had known one of them and he was paroled in the 1990s. His other brother had been in Attica during the riot there in 1971.

There have been other unexpected reunions with ex-cons. Every time, the former inmates would inquire about different staff members who were very fair and respectful toward them. They appreciated the professionalism and consistency of Clinton and how they'd been allowed to simply do their time in that city of concrete and steel.

Bars On the Collar

I simply despised the position of sergeant, which was my motivation to study for lieutenant. Having scored well, I was called shortly after the scores came out. After nearly 16 1/2 months on Staten Island, I once again returned to the Clinton Hub. Approximately another 15 months later, most of it functioning as a captain and Deputy Superintendent for Security at the Lyon Mountain Correctional Facility, I returned to Clinton. My functioning in the capacity of higher ranks more than prepared me for the captain's exam. Not even remotely wanting the position, I wanted to experience the 1/2 written, 1/2 oral interview in front of a panel. I never studied for it but scored well.

While I was still at Lyon Mountain, I had been invited to Clinton Superintendent Ambler's going away party. As a member of my facility's executive team, I was expected to pay homage. Pay homage to this egotistical, vindictive little man? Never, but I wanted to look in his eyes just one more time. My superintendent chuckled at the thought of me going and sighed when he asked, "Can you go without starting something?" I reassured him that I would not put him in that position. I would be a fly on the wall.

I entered the event late, but just in time as Ambler was speaking about how wonderful everyone was and how tough it was to leave. Tough to leave? What a joke! His car sat outside, pointed south and hitched to a trailer. It looked more like a tractor towing a manure spreader and I hoped he was taking all of his bull crap with him. He later made a beeline to me, fumbled with his plate of food, and made a show for all to see – he wanted to shake hands. I must've not been aware of his presence, or I would have been obligated to stand up and shake his hand. It never happened. Not more than a week later, an administrator from another facility that had prepped me for the lieutenant exam laughed as he asked how my legs were. Confused, I told them they were fine. He continued by saying that he heard that they were broken or I would have stood for Ambler. We both started laughing. It had become the administrative wildfire rumor throughout the hub. I got in the last kick. Fuck 'em.

Last Stop – Clinton

Further state budget cuts now forced the closing of the Lyon Mountain Correctional Facility. Superintendent Knox arrived and I sent the officer who had spent that last tour there with me off to his new facility. We were now permanently shut down. I left notes for the superintendent what codes to use and forms to print and where they would need to go. I entered my last entry into the Watch Commander's Log, placed it into the records storage box that I had already properly labeled and sealed it. I was the last Security employee to leave the facility. I drove the 13 miles down Route 374 to Clinton. I was home.

Clinton was not the same place that I had left in May of 2008. There was a different air about the place. The afternoon tour had been without a steady watch commander for over a year, a captain was filling in as an Acting DSS, the other main captain was less than energetic and not pulling his weight. Together, with a new superintendent, this was not a good situation.

Superintendent Little, the latest superintendent, was a longtime Clinton man, but of a different sort. He was short in stature, knowledgeable, and hardworking, but he was not a disciplinarian or a leader. He dreaded receiving a call from his bosses in Albany. The mood at Clinton was very strange. Things were different and there was an air of arrogance amongst the junior staff.

I arrived one morning for overtime and sought out the parking space assigned to the position. A vehicle was parked in the clearly-marked reserved spot. At 9:10 am there is simply nothing available, so I had an announcement made over the facility radios for the owner to call me. When the phone rang, a voice informed me that they owned the vehicle in question. I simply told them that it was an assigned spot, they were to remove it and not to park there anymore. I went back out to move my vehicle which was now blocking others. Upon entering the administration building, a tall, young male officer pointed at me as he approached and angrily challenged, "Ya know, I didn't like the way you spoke to me!" I was puzzled since I didn't even know him, but it was clear that he was the owner of the vehicle.

"You must be the guy with the car." He acknowledged that he was. "What part didn't you like? The part where I told you to not park there again?" Stupefied, he had no response as I chuckled and walked away.

Never in my career had I witnessed so many officers upstairs in the administration building. They would drop into the offices, plop into chairs and flirt with female staff. Even when I was a sergeant, I never wanted to be seen up there. Now it was a common occurrence. Everyone, including the superintendent, saw it, but it had become acceptable behavior. When Clinton had a true administrator in the chair, the staff would scatter when the man came around. We had no leadership.

One afternoon, just before lineup, a junior officer I had never seen before checked in with the sergeant. The young man used a derogatory tone when he addressed the superior and he repeatedly called him by his first name. My fuse had already been lit by some new officers who thought that it was perfectly OK to call higher ranked staff by their first name. No dice. I addressed the lineup about this and did my best to repair the chain of command. I chastised the young staff and later explained to the sergeant that the first name basis makes it, if necessary, tougher to supervise and discipline. I never witnessed it again. The staff felt it was acceptable, since the superintendent was repeatedly being referred to by his first name as well.

The captain's exam scores came out. Only two of Clinton's lieutenants had taken the exam while I was in Lyon Mountain. We had all scored well and the others wanted the promotion badly, despite losing overtime, lineup pay, security, and shift differentials, in exchange for a minimal pay raise. It was a losing proposition for me. The first left for his promotion and the second was nervous as he entered the office I was working in one morning.

Dirk had just left the superintendent's office and asked me, "Little says that you are higher on the captain's list than I am." I reassured him that I had no interest in the promotion and that I had my eyes on boosting my retirement through overtime instead. I made his day and he was promoted to a local facility after I turned it down.

It wasn't long before I was called into the superintendent's office. Superintendent Little and the recently arrived former, filthy captain – now DSS Griese, had been hinting at, but now were asking, if I would be interested in accepting a captain's position at Clinton. I had no interest whatsoever. I was only aware of a single in-house captain promotion and that individual wreaked havoc on the staff. The very first day in his promotion, he had attended the lineups and his message was extremely threatening towards the same staff he'd worked with the day before as a lieutenant. One senior officer in the 2-10 lineup called him out on his threats and ended upstairs after. I simply had no desire for the promotion.

The superintendent and DSS wanted me to take the promotion for all of the wrong reasons. They wanted to send a farewell kick in the ass to the outgoing captain by replacing him with me. They also were hoping to block the one captain who hoped to return. Their deception and hate soured me. They were more interested in grinding personal axes and pursuing vendettas than they were in working together and running the facility. I just didn't trust them. They were looking for a future fall guy, someone to take the blame at times. I refused to be that man.

Dirk was relieved when I refused to accept captain. He was promotion driven and had visions of eagles on his collar. He pulled me into his office and told me that he was glad I turned it down because he didn't want to get into a race for Deputy Superintendent with me. He didn't have to worry about his next promotion after all. Right after the escape, he made a mad dash for retirement. Crap flows downhill and he was at the administration's bottom rung.

What Are The Odds?

My performing schedule was nearly full-time and taking promotions was making it tougher and tougher to juggle both. I worked hard to keep my careers separate, but sometimes it just couldn't be done. A prime example of this was September 16, 2011, when I opened my mailbox.

Imagine my surprise as I discovered a letter from an inmate in the Lansing Correctional Facility in Kansas. After cautiously taking all precautions in opening it, I just could not believe what I was reading. Inmate Ken Haddock - convicted of killing his wife - informed me that his sister had discovered my contact info online and was looking to hire me for my hypnotic skills. Unaware that I was not only a professional hypnotist but also a lieutenant in New York State's largest prison, he outlined his plan to hire me. He was to have a potential witness kidnapped and I was to hypnotize them without their knowledge. The purpose of this was to uncover information that could set him free. As I stood there shaking my head and trying to absorb this, the convict assured me in writing that all of this was perfectly legal. He even provided a self-addressed, stamped envelope for me to correspond with him.

My plate was full and I just didn't want to deal with this lunacy, but I didn't have a choice. I had to report this to the superintendent. The next day was a Saturday and I was working a double shift as watch commander in the Main. I wrote my report, made copies, and when time allowed, called the prison in Kansas to make them aware. I was put in contact with a staff member who monitored him and he was blown away by

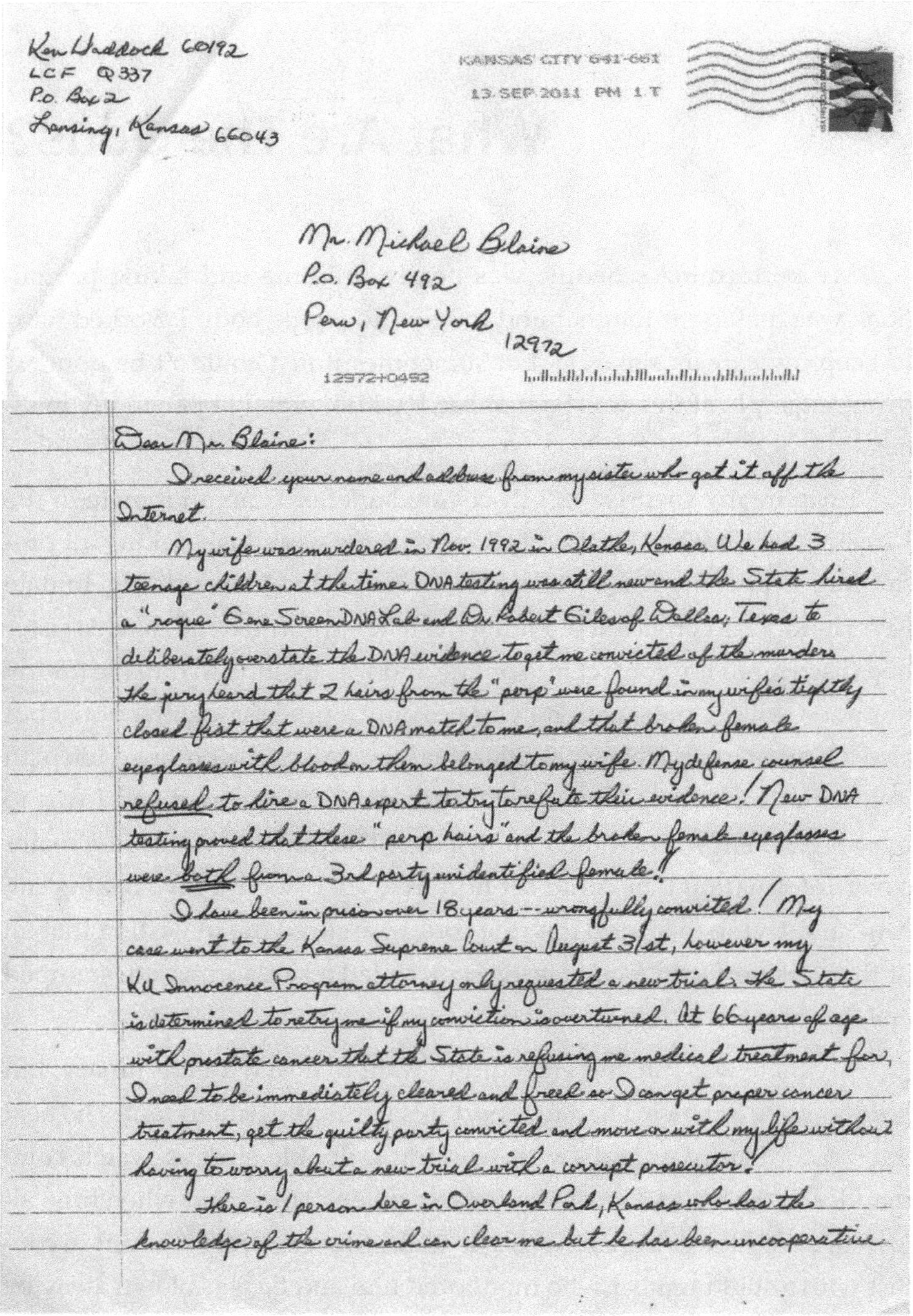

Ken Waddock 60192
LCF Q337
P.O. Box 2
Lansing, Kansas 66043

KANSAS CITY 641-661
13 SEP 2011 PM 1 T

Mr. Michael Blaine
P.O. Box 492
Peru, New York 12972

12972+0492

Dear Mr. Blaine:

I received your name and address from my sister who got it off the Internet.

My wife was murdered in Nov. 1992 in Olathe, Kansas. We had 3 teenage children at the time. DNA testing was still new and the State hired a "rogue" Gene Screen DNA Lab and Dr. Robert Giles of Dallas, Texas to deliberately overstate the DNA evidence to get me convicted of the murder. The jury heard that 2 hairs from the "perp" were found in my wife's tightly closed fist that were a DNA match to me, and that broken female eyeglasses with blood on them belonged to my wife. My defense counsel refused to hire a DNA expert to try to refute their evidence! New DNA testing proved that these "perp hairs" and the broken female eyeglasses were both from a 3rd party unidentified female!

I have been in prison over 18 years -- wrongfully convicted! My case went to the Kansas Supreme Court on August 31st, however my KU Innocence Program attorney only requested a new trial; the State is determined to retry me if my conviction is overturned. At 66 years of age with prostate cancer that the State is refusing me medical treatment for, I need to be immediately cleared and freed so I can get proper cancer treatment, get the guilty party convicted and move on with my life without having to worry about a new trial with a corrupt prosecutor!

There is 1 person here in Overland Park, Kansas who has the knowledge of the crime and can clear me but he has been uncooperative

Letter addressed to the author from an inmate in Kansas

the letter. I faxed him a copy of what I had received and he looked into it. We made contact again a few days later and he shared his discussion with Haddock. He explained that Haddock initially denied contacting any hypnotists or proposing any plan as I had described. When confronted with the fact that he had indeed not only contacted a hypnotist, but he actually had sent his plan to a New York State Peace Officer, the look on his face was priceless! You just can't make this stuff up!

Merle Cooper Program

Another sign of Clinton's decline was Albany removing two of the best programs I had ever seen implemented in New York State. Located in the Annex, these programs were known as the "Merle Cooper Program." Its furniture shop employed a number of the inmates involved in the therapeutic program. The housing units associated with this program were not only clean and orderly, but they were also vastly more productive and relatively problem-free, unlike general population housing units and programs.

Merle Cooper had been a long-time business officer for Dannemora State Hospital who had died in the 1970s. In 1977, a voluntary program named for him was initiated that focused on inmates who had difficulty adjusting to life in and out of prison and were given therapeutic, community-intensive, long-term counseling. These inmates, for the most part, were very clean and polite, despite the intermingling of some very unusual individuals who could never survive in the general population. Members of the program lived, worked, ate, and recreated separately from the rest of the Annex population.

Uniformed officers functioned as counselors in conjunction with civilian counselors and psychologists. Community meetings involved inmates sitting in a circle with one inmate sitting on the "hot seat" in the middle, on display and for all to see and hear. It was here that the inmate was to talk about his life, crime, misdeeds and whatever issues others might have with him. Nothing was off-limits and you could hear a pin drop when things got intense. The sharks would circle and jump at their chance to verbally confront their fellow inmate in a group setting. I only observed a few of these meetings, but the much more senior officers would laugh in private over some of the more outlandish stories they had heard over the years: wild stories of one inmate having engaged in sex with a horse while on the street, another extorting other weaker inmates, homosexual behavior, stealing, etc. It all came out in these meetings as the offender was forced to address the accusations.

The furniture shop was the most positive, highest-producing single program I had ever witnessed in the department. The shop produced both beautiful wooden and vinyl lettered signs for whatever agency or facility requested them. Over the years, they produced toys for charitable groups, repaired and re-finished facility furniture, as well as countless other projects. The numerous, high-quality benches and picnic tables at the Clinton County Fairgrounds, a mere 12 miles from the facility, stand today as a testimony to its productivity. The late 1990s, when a decent chair in the facility could not be had, saw security staff liberating chairs from civilian areas after business hours, or during a weekend or holiday while they were away. After all, their departmental budgets would allow them to simply order another, while officers were forced to work with what he had. The shop was directed to mass-produce a large number of very comfortable and functional chairs, and they did. This was all done with one civilian instructor, one officer and a handful of very cooperative and appreciative inmates from the Merle Cooper Program. They truly appreciated the opportunity to get away from the housing unit and the sense of accomplishment. There is simply no way the state could ever justify shutting down such a positive, productive program, but they did. Many inmates wrote letters opposing the closure and the housing units were quickly converted to general population units. Captain Caught quickly planned on shuffling the deck and relocated the mess hall inmates into these very clean and private units. This was the most idiotic maneuver ever. Why? Most mess hall workers were assigned that job when they finish a disciplinary disposition for misbehavior. Plus, less disciplined means were problematic and unhygienic. Finally, inmates transferring into the facility were assigned as needed. If the facility needs mess hall workers, and they always do, that is where they go. Captain Caught fought hard to make this happen over my countless objections to him and Superintendent Little. They had their marching orders from their Albany masters and no arguments were strong enough to demonstrate the value of such a program. The dysfunction of the administration and the department overall was absolutely overwhelming and there was no reasoning with them.

A Train Running Off Its Tracks

My last position in Clinton allowed me to have greater access to overtime and shift swaps. I was in my last years and I continued to burn the candle at both ends. I was worn out and getting swaps for time away to perform was becoming tougher and tougher. The other lieutenants were older and tough to nail down for committed dates. It was becoming frustrating dealing with the former lieutenant caught-with-his-pants-down, now captain. He was a strange and unusual man. Everything that happened was somehow my fault. The more he blamed on me, the more I laughed. Even if I was two thousand miles away, anything askew just had to be of my doing. He was nuts and jealous.

The poor guy seemed to have more issues than *Reader's Digest*. He became upset when I ordered his secretary out of my office. She was loud and carried on personal conversations with staff while I worked as if the office were her own. This was the same secretary that reeked of cheap perfume, who would schmooze the other lieutenants as they allowed her to take the facility count. I made it clear to all that if I witnessed this for myself, I was going to the very top with it. The captain – Captain Caught – was well aware of this practice and yet he allowed it.

In my 26+ years, I had never worked for anyone with crappier judgment. When a male officer was caught being hugged by an inmate, the investigation began. I was ordered to interview the inmate and I detailed my findings. The inmate openly admitted to hugging the officer. As I questioned him, he openly stated, "We had a type of father/son relationship." Floored, I reported back to Captain Caught and he undoubtedly swept this unauthorized behavior under the rug. The officer was a perpetual screwup and it wasn't long before he locked himself in the housing unit staff bathroom, refusing to come out. Captain Caught was seen carrying out the contraband personal property – which included makeup – of the employee out of the facility so he could give it to him.

More of his skewed judgment became apparent when he buried an investigation into an employee showing signs of having been corrupted. I had reliable, confidential information regarding an employee bringing in contraband, food, paint, and other items for inmates. I had staff search for and retrieve an item of contraband as verification. They did and I now had the answers that I needed to pass this on for an IG investigation. Captain Caught simply scoffed, opened his bottom desk drawer, and dropped it in. He had stated openly in the past that he liked the employee. I now wonder that if Captain Caught had actually done his job and disciplined the employee, would Joyce Mitchell, Gene Palmer, and the others have taken notice and changed their ways?

I had refused a promotion to captain twenty-two times. Only once had I considered, and accepted, a position in Albany that I had been recruited for, but I refused it a few weeks later so I could wrap up with my last year's overtime boost. This drove my captain crazy. Ever since I refused to do his work for him anymore, he had constantly attacked me. He was unaware that, pursuant to departmental directives, I could not and would no longer do his work for him. Clearly shocked, he slithered away to research the information. He plotted and planned, waiting for me to say a single word that he did not approve of. He created the most outlandish tales and called me on his carpet to chastise me. I couldn't win. I didn't even try – until one day.

I was called into his office and he began berating me. The lies were growing with every word he spoke. He was simply beside himself as he accused me of everything under the sun. I refused to take it anymore. I simply told him that he was a liar. He increased his attack and I told him that he was a "fucking liar." He challenged me with, "Anything else you want to say?" I said, "Yes. You're a fucking liar and you're incompetent." That clearly struck a nerve with him. He began to work the phone and I was ordered to the superintendent's office.

Captain Caught-with-his-pants-down began his laundry list of grievances against me. Superintendent Little asked me if I had made the statements and I admitted that I had. He asked me why and I told him that I wouldn't be falsely accused. The meeting ended up with Captain Caught madder and even more determined to try to screw me over. I warned the superintendent that this wasn't over… and it wasn't.

Superintendent Little was summoned to the Central Office. They had had enough of him and Clinton's mismanagement. He was being replaced right there and then. On the personnel change notice, his Item Number (a type of facility employment ID number) had been demoted to captain and he was transferred to another facility. He refused to accept the voluntary demotion and he left state service. The new superintendent had a reputation of being fair as a leader, but I just wanted out. I had seen

STATE OF NEW YORK – DEPARTMENT OF CORRECTIONS
AND COMMUNITY SUPERVISION
CLINTON CORRECTIONAL FACILITY

Interdepartmental Communication

FROM: Jill Besaw, Head Clerk Personnel *Jill Besaw*

TO: Steven Racette, Superintendent

SUBJECT: Personnel Changes

DATE: **March 19, 2014**

00101 Steven Racette, Superintendent @ Upstate – Permanent reassignment to Clinton as Superintendent in item #00101, effective 3/17/14.

00101 [redacted], Superintendent – Reassign Permanent Captain hold from Clinton's Correction Captain item #10002 to a Permanent hold on Adirondack's Correction Captain item #10001 effective 3/13/14.

The order reassigning Clinton administrative personnel

Clinton change too much over the years. It wasn't the same place anymore.

Captain Caught had no idea that my plan had been set into motion a year earlier. All of his allegations against me weren't worth the paper he wrote them on. He had pressed me for my plans and I refused to disclose them. The plan was simple: work my butt off and walk away with a retirement that he could only dream of. I left for knee surgery, and, while recovering, I filed my retirement papers on an absolutely gorgeous day in May. Following my light duty assignment, as I recuperated, I reported for my last two days of work.

The author in front of the facility announcement board at his retirement

I made that last drive to Clinton as an employee on the morning of July 24, 2014. I eased up the road to the personnel office on my 2013 Harley Street Glide. I had purchased that particular model year as a reminder that I was eligible to retire that year. I have it to this day.

I was now free of uniforms, rules, and regulations, working countless double shifts, mandatory overtime, and scams by inmates and also staff. No more watching staff inform on each other. No more scowls as I come to work happy, with a spring in my step. It was over, or was it?

The Escape That Could Not Happen

I awoke to a series of text messages from Ed. He went on and on, detailing the escape of two cons from A Block. I chuckled at his attempt to put one over on me. Cut through the back of a cell? A pipe? Out a manhole cover? Impossible!

The messages were simply much too detailed and excited to not confirm. I pulled up the local TV station and newspaper websites and there was no mention of anything of the sort. I opened up my Facebook and it was bombarded with information. "Holy shit. This really happened. How could it happen? Impossible!" My mind simply would not accept that not only did one convict escape but two!

Like everyone else in the North Country, I was glued to the media for updates. For the first time in my life, I now armed myself when I left the house. The region was gripped with fear, and rightfully so. I recalled the profiles of inmates Matt and Sweat while working occasionally as the Safety and Security Lieutenant prior to my retiring in July 2014, just ten and a half months before this event. Both of these men were of the CMC-A classification. The Central Monitoring Case designation and the letter dictated that these inmates were to be very closely monitored. These were dangerous men with nothing to lose and everything to gain.

Governor Cuomo rushed to scene and it baffled us that he was allowing photos of a very sensitive nature to be made public. He reported to the antiquated Command Center that had been set up and promptly ordered the Clinton County Sheriff out of the room. He wanted to meet with his boys. Despite being the ultimate law enforcement authority within the County, the sheriff complied. The governor was trying to look like a leader and he was clearly calling the shots.

The hearts of the public went out to the guys in the field. Photos of ripped boots hit the media and a call to action for supplies and donations was sounded. Many of us rounded up supplies for the searchers. I had dropped off my first load at the Saranac Fire Station and saw many Albany CERT members milling about in clean, comfortable conditions. It was clear that they were being well taken care of, so I informed many to divert the supplies to the Quality of Work Life building at the facility instead, where the guys who were working would get much needed insect repellent, sunblock, baby wipes, and food items, as well as bottled water that they could fill their pockets with while working the insane hours demanded of them.

The media machine grasped at any rumor and filled the airwaves with completely fabricated lines of shit. Anyone with any basic knowledge of the facility simply could not stomach all of the lies. One evening I received a phone call from New York City. A producer from CBS news had somehow located me via the retirement system and wanted to speak with me. I agreed. The reporter and her people would meet me at my house in an hour.

We sat in my formal living room and talked over a drink. They were amazed at what I had to say about the mismanagement of the facility prior to the removal of the previous superintendent in the spring of 2014. I went on about how I had brought numerous issues to his attention and his response was always the same: "I'll put out a memo." This guy simply did not understand what leadership was about. "You are at the top, tell your people what you want done and it will filter down. Hold people accountable for their actions." He simply would not listen and I would leave his office even more frustrated at his lack of leadership.

"May we put you on the record and record you?" they excitedly asked. I refused and they then offered to change my voice and tape me in silhouette. I again refused. "May we at least use you for story accuracy?" That much I agreed to and starting the next day they were sending me the most outlandish stories, which I told them were just plain bullshit. Sometimes they would have little mistakes and I would explain other things to them. Their stories were becoming more and more accurate. It didn't take long for other networks to discover me as well.

The author interviewed by the media during the 2015 escape

One network asked me to do an interview in the early afternoon. The producers and I repeatedly went over what I could and could not discuss. Live from a studio in Albany, I listened through an earpiece and looked into a camera. The well-known, blonde newscaster clearly had no idea what she was talking about and immediately went for sensitive security information. I avoided her question and was livid. Everyone who knew me and watched it live said the very same thing: "Boy, were you pissed off!" Indeed I was. I lost all respect for the media on that day.

The networks continued to pull in anyone who would speak with them, including ex-cons. The line of bullshit that they were letting one spew was transparent. This ex-con, in a matter of a few weeks, went from calling the escapees, "Inmates Matt and Sweat" to "Matt and Sweat," then "Rich and Dave." The networks never caught on that this little man had recently been rearrested and his case went before the Grand Jury, but he was not indicted. He was a self-serving, attention-seeking con looking to make some cash off the escape. Sure, he might have known and worked with these two, but "lifers" - inmates with life sentences - do not typically want other inmates with short sentences around them. He had been at Clinton due to his poor disciplinary history. He was the type who would draw attention to himself and would have much to gain by informing or "ratting" on Matt and Sweat. He was, more than likely, scared to death of those two.

I stopped by the farm of Keith, an officer who had retired before me as I was passing by on my Harley. One of the most straightforward men from Clinton, I valued his input. He was sitting on his tailgate, spitting tobacco as I pulled in. Even with my sunglasses and helmet, he recognized my smile. As I approached, I pointed at him and said, "You would have known." He spat onto the ground and replied, "Ya know, I wonder if I would have. I had some pretty damn good rats in that block." We spoke at length about the ordeal and our disgust with the entire situation was mutual.

My friend, a fellow Freemason and Shriner from western Canada, owned a beautiful camp on Lake Titus. He reached out to me, saying that he felt like a prisoner in his own place. Everyone was armed and the area was swarming with law enforcement. At night, if they heard a sound outside and went near a window, the house would be lit up with searchlights. They simply could not get any rest and were itching for some company or just to get out of the search area. Inmate Matt had been shot dead the day before and the region was buzzing. We agreed to meet the next day, a Sunday, if we were allowed into the region.

We met and had the most wonderful visit over lunch. None of us were in a hurry and we chatted for a few hours in a little diner in Mountain View, New York. My friend and his wife dreaded the thought of returning to their fortress. Suddenly, a text message came across my phone with a simple message: "Sweat captured. No other info." I interrupted the chatter with the info and people wanted details. We turned the TV in the diner to the news channel and it was apparent that they had no clue about the capture.

I forwarded the message to my media contacts. They instantly responded. One had been on their way to Vermont to conduct an interview. They spun around and raced to Constable, New York, to get the scoop. They asked if I was in the area and I said that I was, so they asked me to do interviews about the escape and I agreed. Outside of the Alice Hyde Hospital, I was asked about the capture and I expressed the relief the region felt. The incident was over, but only the search itself was over. So much more lay ahead that would never be brought to light.

It was a day that we should not have needed to celebrate. The escape should never have happened. Our trust in Gene Palmer and Joyce Mitchell was violated, along with that placed in many others who were never charged. It was the greatest slap in the face to anyone who had worked at and took pride in their job at Clinton. This chapter was over but so much more remained.

Gene and Joyce Go to Jail

The facts were not yet public, but Gene Palmer had been arrested. My heart went out to my friend of 29 years. I'd seen him at the local county fair in July 2015, where he was scheduled to perform. After my last performance of the night, I sought him out. He and his band were finishing their set and took a break. I walked up to him and shook hands. He and I spoke as he got changed, with him repeatedly cursing inmates Matt and Sweat.

Gene was allowed to plead guilty to one count of promoting prison contraband in the 2nd degree, a misdemeanor, one count of promoting prison contraband in the 1st degree, a felony, and a felony count of official misconduct. He was sentenced to six months in the Clinton County Jail.

I wrote to Gene as a longtime friend while he was in jail. At this point, many of us believed that he had been an unknowing participant and was duped by Joyce Mitchell. I was concerned about his adjustment and well-being. He responded in a timely manner, but his reply upset me a great deal. Although I will not reveal the letter's contents, I was upset when he played the role of the innocent. Some of his final words in the letter thanked me for not turning my back on him. I wrote back, informing him that I had simply written to him as a longtime friend and that I did not, in any way, condone anything that had taken place. He never wrote back after that.

I hadn't turned my back on Gene because I wasn't aware of his actions. A lot of information in the final report revealed many of his unauthorized activities. The paintings, favors, introduction of contraband, and other actions were alarming enough, but I, along with countless others, felt even more betrayed and violated when we saw the group photo of the four officers in A Block, which had been taken by an inmate using Gene's cell phone. The photo appeared in the IG report and hit the media. I felt even more violated by the report's author, who tried to use this an example of widespread corruption in Clinton, as well as by Gene who claimed it was the only time he had ever taken his cell phone into the facility.

I would have never believed that Gene would engage in such misconduct. That photo, the smug looks, the relaxed poses, the paintings, the favors, and the betrayal would all soon be revealed. It cut deep, even if you had been retired for years. The report would put salt on the wounds of so many by suggesting that this was a common practice amongst staff. This could not be any further from the truth. I had worked with some of the best in the business. As difficult as it was to believe that Clinton officers committed these acts, I turned my back then as well.

The photo with Gene Palmer taken in A bock from the IG report

I have already pointed out examples of corrupted and jeopardized staff. It happens throughout the system and in every occupation, in every walk of life. However, the insinuation that Clinton was a den of widespread misconduct is completely false. During my career, the IG investigators themselves were caught screwing the pooch by padding their per diem. Their incompetence was demonstrated in failing to properly investigate Joyce Mitchell, immediately searching the inmate's property and cell, and transferring the inmate. This incident could have been nipped in the bud. They own their fair share of it.

Joyce Mitchell copped a plea as well. She was sentenced on September 28, 2015, and I was there when she was escorted out of the building. The media was marking their territory, but I stood my ground. I wanted to see her in restraints. As they escorted her out from the Clinton County Government Center, she looked down and shuffled along, nearly tripping on the chain from the leg irons resting secured above her ankles, just like she did on her way out of the courtroom. I had the perfect spot and I took advantage of it by calling out, "They're gonna love you in Bedford (Hills)… a lot!"

I created the Facebook page, "Voice Against Joyce." The purpose is to keep the public informed of inmate Joyce Mitchell's parole hearings and to organize letter-writing campaigns. The most recent campaign was instrumental in generating hundreds of letters voicing their opposition to her release. Each letter must be read, be determined to be for or against the parole, and copied for each board member. This creates some serious added duty for staff. Unfortunately, Joyce was ultimately released from prison in February, 2020.

The Escape Report

The escape left everyone looking for cover. The state was looking for someone to blame and nobody was safe. The Deputy Superintendent for Security in the report denied any knowledge of the midnight shift counts being collected beforehand. The report cites his statement:

"Should [it surprise me], no. Unfortunately, no. We don't do a frickin' thing on midnights except for manning a round. I don't know why you would have to fill out your count list [in advance], but could see people doing it, yes."

"I should have known if it was. I would have told them don't do it."

This statement leaves many questions unanswered. How can this administrator make the claim that "We don't do a frickin' thing on midnights except for manning a round," without having firsthand knowledge of the facility? This same man had worked Clinton as an officer, sergeant, lieutenant, captain, and then finally as the Deputy Superintendent for Security, and he claims to have no knowledge? Seriously?

The report also contained findings about the inaction by the superintendent in 2012 in regards to Joyce Mitchell. He had dreaded grievances and repeatedly failed to act on issues. He preferred the wait and see approach, hoping the issue would resolve itself. It seemed that the word "proactive" was not in his vocabulary. The report reveals that a number of people had taken issue with her attire but it was clearly never addressed. The report stated:

DOCCS policy states that civilian employees "shall be... appropriately dressed while on duty" and "must be dressed in neat, clean attire that is in good repair and not revealing or extremely tight-fitting."

The irony is that this is one of the many issues that I, as a lieutenant, had personally brought to the attention of the superintendent at nearly the same exact time. I described to him in detail the revealing clothing and open shoes that female civilian staff wore throughout the facility. He agreed that it was improper, but he did nothing.

One of the greatest lies sold to the public regarding the escape was the pipe itself. The public was somehow supposed to believe that Sweat, using a hacksaw blade, made perfectly straight cuts, entered the pipe, and then cut his way out from the inside. Countless rumors circulated throughout the North Country that an administrator was in possession of documentation proving that the cut was actually done by a contractor. Not having been paid by the state, they picked up their tools and never completed the project. This was an ongoing issue throughout the state since bills were never paid on time.

Shortly after the escape, security staff were present as workers removed the compromised pipe from outside of the prison wall. Captain Caught entered the work area and ordered those present to sign a confidentiality statement. It soon became apparent why. The pipe was clearly cut from the outside. The chalk markings clearly outlined where the cuts were to be made. This went against the official report.

Other issues were kept quiet and hidden from the public. After a facility-wide check, a number of cells had to be taken out of service due because the bottoms of the steel walls could be pushed out. Repairs were made and the cells put back into service.

This escape was the product of a perfect storm. It could have never occurred without employee assistance. Countless staff had made comments just prior to the escape that the facility had actually been running smoother with the current superintendent at the helm. As one employee said, "You could feel it. The staff were pulling together and taking it upon themselves to get things done. You could feel the place making a turn in the right direction again." You simply don't turn a place like Clinton on a dime and this man had been thrown into a huge mess.

Additional Escape Info

After the escape, the truth about it began to leak out from those who were there that morning and during the following days.

The staff at Clinton were aghast at the interference of Governor Cuomo as he insisted on pushing his way into the escape investigation. Eyewitnesses detailed the entrance of the governor and his security detail into the facility with their phones and weapons. The introduction of weapons and electronic devices into a correctional facility was a dangerous and unnecessary maneuver and was interpreted as a complete disregard for all staff. According to one officer, a state police employee – informed the governor that he should not enter the area due to it being an active crime scene. The governor did as he wished and the employee wasn't seen at Clinton again after that day, but rumors abounded that he had hastily retired.

Staff repeatedly expressed total contempt for the official escape report. The evidence at the manhole cover didn't support the claim that the two escapees exited from there. It was the great wisdom of the governor that made that determination. It appears that he ignored the evidence and probability that the inmates made their way through the tunnel all the way down to and out of the powerhouse since the gate at the end of the tunnel had swung unsecured for quite some time. A source that was very involved with the escape fallout and who had personally witnessed a great deal filled me in that an elderly woman that lived at the manhole intersection had been watching TV in her kitchen at the time the inmates would have exited the manhole. The next day she heard the sound of metal scraping on the pavement as the cover was removed and was shocked to learn of the escape. It was not until nearly two weeks later that she was finally interviewed. She insisted that if they had moved the cover during the night as alleged, she would have heard it.

One source explained that there is no doubt in his mind that they simply walked out through the powerhouse. After all, the security gates had been removed years earlier and they had a clear line all the way to the powerhouse. He described the lax security in the powerhouse. When the opportune moment presented itself, the escapees could have slipped past any staff working, disappearing into the night, where Joyce Mitchell would have been waiting for them.

Speculation by staff regarding holes in the back walls of the escapees' cells does have validity. Some buy the story claiming they were cut with a hacksaw blade, but others believe that they had assistance. One senior staff member offered the theory that the inmates could have quite possibly recognized a laborer from a civilian work crew from the street or made their acquaintance. All contractors and staff are supposed to undergo a thorough background check, which would prohibit suspicious persons from having access to the facility. However, quite often, the background checks from Albany were slow. When eventually discovered, the suspicious persons were escorted off the grounds. Years earlier, while at Lyon Mountain Correctional Facility, I received a call from the Clinton Safety and Security Lieutenant directing me to remove a laborer from a project at my facility due to his criminal background. Imagine my surprise when I heard the name and sought out this former correction officer who I had worked with many years earlier. I relayed the message and he packed up and left.

Knowing that so much construction and renovation was taking place, the noise of power tools cutting metal emitting from the catwalk area in A-Block would not arouse suspicion. The amount of cutting that these two allegedly did on their own was incredible and would have required a heck of a lot more than just a few hacksaw blades. It is not unreasonable at all to entertain the possibility of some assistance in this manner.

Lights, Camera, Action!

Ben Stiller was in the area looking to do a movie about the escape. The region was very divided over the project. Social media was abuzz and some resented having to relive the escape. The locations for filming were chosen, and calls for extras were made. They were being given unprecedented access to Clinton. Clinton's staff were, at times, prevented from entering the facility's property on time for work due to filming. It appeared that as long as they stuck to the official escape report story, they could do as they pleased.

One network had already done a poorly produced show about Joyce Mitchell and it made everyone skeptical about this project. Word soon spread that this one was to be as authentic as possible. It was now March and the movie had more shooting to do in Clinton County. More notices for extras were announced and I answered one. I wasn't available for the original call, but I was for the second.

At the very end of filming, I was called to play the role of my first job as a lieutenant at Clinton - afternoon watch commander. I reported to the Orange County Jail as directed and was sent through the jail to the gym, where I would witness many aspects of the film industry.

An advisor for the movie was the same retired captain that Superintendent Little and DSS Griese had asked me to replace. He filled me in that they were striving for authenticity, a major concern for me. I then checked in and the process began after I filled out my payment paperwork.

Wardrobe was at one end of the room, with racks and racks of costume uniforms for all aspects of the movie. All law enforcement agencies,

Paper badge worn by the author on the set of *Escape at Dannemora*

inmates, etc. Once you were given your costume, it was time try it on, get it tailored and sit around and wait. I met extras from all walks of life: teachers, retired cops, even a federal correction officer who was sent to the barber chair. When he emerged, he was sporting a shorter haircut and was without his prominent red goatee, which he was clearly embarrassed about.

They were all shocked to learn that I had actually worked at and retired from Clinton. They had a pile of questions and we all shared a few laughs as we had an incredible catered lunch, waited, and made small talk. The film crew, actors and the staff, including Ben Stiller, sat down and ate and we headed to get the necessary props for our rank roles. Then we were off to the set.

We entered the room that was to serve as the Clinton Watch Commander's office. It was less than half the size of what it should be. They walked us through what the scene was and we awaited the arrival of Mr. Stiller. When he arrived, he realized that it was much too crowded and he thinned out the extras. After another walkthrough, I was removed by him as well.

Those who were not being used in the scene were allowed to watch from outside. It was incredible to see what it would look like on the screen. After a few takes, it wrapped up. Despite being disappointed that the scene wasn't authentic, I was impressed with the foresight used to create it and how cool it looked. That all ended after the first five minutes of the first episode.

The Miniseries

Right from the start, Stiller's series, which was supposed to be as "authentic as possible," demonstrated that it was not going to be mistaken with the phrase as "accurate as possible." Prior to its release for the public, the Inspector General reviewed the entire series and authorized it to be aired.

The series was dark, slow, and drawn out. If one had no knowledge of Clinton or the North Country, they would believe that every employee was an obese, slovenly, corrupt abuser of inmates. The only thing about Clinton that was properly represented was the North Yard. In a few scenes, visible in the background is the wall post that I had fired from in 1998.

The depiction of staff as lowlifes who spat into the face of an inmate dragged batons across cell bars and engaged in unwarranted baton use on compliant inmates in the yard, offended not only myself but also a legion of past and present staff. As the series unfolded, it became clear that it had a deliberate anti-authority, left-leaning agenda. It was almost as if Governor Cuomo wanted to demean and degrade the staff within the walls of Clinton and was using this director to do it.

One thing that I was glad to see in the series were the subtle hints at the involvement of Gene Palmer's red-haired girlfriend in the background, one of the many mysteries of the escape.

If Palmer was referred to as "The Mayor" in A-Block, she would have been his second-in-command and he would do whatever it took to protect her. If she had an issue with a supervisor, as she did with me when I was a sergeant in 2007, Gene would run interference, just like he did when I attempted to verbally counsel her on her continued violations of rules and regulations. Her biggest shield to hide behind was the allegation of harassment. The counseling session proved futile. Word spread like wildfire, and while working as the Annex Chart Sergeant during the latter part of my double shift that day, my watch commander let on that he knew about what had happened. He urged me to report it in writing to then-Deputy Superintendent for Security, Steve Racette, the same man who would be the superintendent of Clinton during the escape!

As the midnight watch commander, the Security Lieutenant from the day shift working overtime took over, he called me aside to ask a favor of me. He didn't even get the chance to start talking when I asked, "Gene wants me to drop this?" He indicated that he did. I told him that I would, but I wanted word to get back to his woman that if she ever acted like that again towards me I would push the discipline as far as I could. He agreed and I took the paperwork home with me. I was shocked to learn after the escape and learning of their involvement that I was still in possession of that very same paperwork.

When I wrote to Gene in the Clinton County Jail, it was because I was unaware of the facts and I was genuinely concerned about his adjustment from C.O. to C-O-N. Had I known of his true involvement and his delusional activities that ultimately jeopardized thousands of residents and hundreds of searchers, I would have turned my back on him much earlier. Like most of my fellow correctional employees, we depend on one another and loyalty means everything. We do not take betrayal lightly. Some wounds will never heal.

Clinton will never be the same. A few self-serving, delusional employees who got caught up in their fantasy worlds caused irreparable harm to a prison in northern New York State that had withstood the test of time. Clinton held the worst that the state could produce, and shielded the outside world with its gray, foreboding wall with thousands and thousands of feet of concrete, only to fall victim to two convicts in an 18-inch pipe beneath it.

Undisclosed To The Public

The extortion attempt by Matt

For years, inmate Richard Matt and the other CMC-designated inmates were properly monitored by the Safety and Security Lieutenant. Around late 2011, early 2012, Matt came under suspicion of attempting to extort a female civilian in Tailor 2. The female was upset when she discovered a note that had been slipped through the vent louvre of her locker. The note was typewritten and threatened to expose her for allegedly bringing some items in for another inmate unless she did so for them as well.

The civilian did exactly as she was supposed to do: she alerted security staff and the supervisors investigated. The civilian was extremely cooperative and was cleared of any wrongdoing in record time. The shop inmates were interviewed, cells searched, and clues sought as to the identity of the author. The typewriter that had been used had a letter that that was a little off. The search was on, but the specific typewriter could not be found.

Matt was interviewed by the lieutenant himself. Armed with confidential sources implicating Matt, he also had Matt's background, arrests, convictions, profile, and disciplinary record, which indicated similar past behavior. The interrogation began. Cool as a cucumber, this career criminal wouldn't be cracked. He clearly knew how to cover his tracks. Maybe the lieutenant couldn't pin it on Matt, but he could remove him from the Industry Building and with it Matt's highly-desired tailor shops for security reasons – and he did. Matt was not to be assigned to the shops for any reason. Officer Tina Barker dutifully entered the information into the computer system as directed. It was set in stone until October 31, 2013, when that lieutenant retired. It is obvious that someone with the right computer access and codes removed the designation after he left state service. Who had authorized its removal? Why hadn't the Inspector General searched for the footprint in the computer system to find out who had made the change?

Inmate Matt should have never even been near Joyce Mitchell in 2015. Had the notes not been removed from the computer, he never would have even met her.

The Tunnels

Just like a vast majority of Clinton's staff, I had never been in the tunnels. For the most part, only experienced, senior staff were utilized for inspections. After all, people talk and cons listen.

The inspections were conducted on a monthly basis until the mid-1990s. It was at that time that the tunnels were deemed confined space and the inspections were cut back to an annual inspection, in addition to after any emergency. Following the escape, regular inspections were implemented, but for security reasons, I will not disclose the intervals. Internal sources have detailed the elaborate security measures that now secure the tunnel system. It took Clinton from the medieval to the futuristic in a matter of months. Nobody will ever escape through those tunnels again.

The Pipe

The pipefitters confirmed what everyone already knew: the nice, neat, well-marked entry hole into the pipe was never cut by hand. They also dispelled another theory: it wasn't a plasma cutter either since there wasn't any slag (small pieces of waste matter) present. Working 24 hours a day for more than three days, the breached pipe was removed. The 18-inch high-grade steel pipe, with a thickness of 3/8", was cut into a section approximately 8 to 12 feet in length and removed. The replacement was triple welded into place.

The Manhole Cover

Among the many details about the escape that never made it to the public concerned the manhole cover that Matt and Sweat escaped through. The manhole covers had been chained to the ladder beneath them and locked. As the manhole in question was inspected, it was discovered that approximately six toe and fingernail clippers had been used to wedge the manhole cover up from underneath. The top link of the chain had been cut, thus allowing the cover to be removed. Logic dictates that wedging from below, creating the slightest opening so that the top link - up close to the cover itself - could be cut, means that it was cut from outside the manhole! The escaping inmates could have easily cut the bottom link securing it to the ladder inside. It would have been incredibly difficult for them to work a blade at the top. The investigators did not want any part of this theory and it was quickly swept away.

The Camp

In an effort to sensationalize the scenes with the hunting camp, where the inmates were discovered and gave the searchers their first confirmed sighting, the mini-series suggested that Sweat had found a pistol laying around when there wasn't any. The shotgun Matt found was a simple, single-shot, and not the pump shotgun utilized on the screen. There was no running water or indoor plumbing.

Clinton Today

The knee-jerk reaction to the escape by Governor Cuomo has resulted in a flood of money and changing policies and procedures seemingly intended to degrade anyone who was employed in corrections. Staff throughout the state are now required to use the small, see-through, clear plastic totes that are jokingly referred to as the "Palmer Pack" or the "Tilly Tote." Body cams are now utilized and thousands of cameras are now in use within the facility. Discipline has been eroded by liberal lawsuits. The last resort tool of discipline for inmates, nutri-loaf and cabbage, has been eliminated. Offenses that used to elicit a disposition of 12-18 months in the SHU now get 6 or less. The liberal lunatics are running the asylum.

SHU 200's, modernized Special Housing Units, are being closed down at a record pace. These problematic inmates are being put back into the general population with junior and inexperienced staff. It is a recipe for disaster.

Nearly all of the staffing issues that we battled throughout my career were now suddenly, magically solved. Wall posts and other positions that were closed or partially closed are now fully staffed. Unfortunately, staff are now targets and people have retired in droves in an attempt to get away from the madness. The facilities are no longer what they were during my career. Discipline now seems to be only for the employees.

Inmate misbehavior discipline guidelines have been completely rewritten. The facilities are loaded with inexperienced staff. Female officers are now regularly attacked by inmates. This was unthinkable just a few years earlier.

Even at the training academy, the recruits are fed a steady diet of anti-Clinton rhetoric. Everything is Clinton's fault; all Clinton staff are corrupt. Total nonsense, but it is the tone set by the governor. The Albany employees are more puppet-like than they have ever been. I guess we could point the finger right back at them for producing less-than-acceptable officers who, according to Clinton's old-timers, have no concept of respect and no desire to learn how jailing is done.

One retiree explained that following the escape, he met with an administrator he had known for quite some time. He explained that he told them that someone was going to get killed. The operation of the facility and the new staff were simply too dangerous to remain.

Even after the escape from Clinton, the killing of inmate Matt, the capture of Sweat, and pleas by Palmer and Mitchell, the sheer stupidity of staff willingly dealing with and assisting inmates continues. Denise Prell, a female tailor shop civilian hired after the escape, who was arrested in October 2017, rejected a plea deal of a single felony count of Promoting Prison Contraband. Taking her chances with a grand jury, she was indicted on March 15, 2018, on 1st Degree charges of Promoting Prison Contraband, 3rd Degree Sexual Abuse, and 23 counts of official misconduct. She later pled to Promoting Prison Contraband in the 2nd degree, 23 counts of official misconduct, and one count of sexual abuse in the 3rd degree - all misdemeanors. She was sentenced to two 1 year sentences in the county jail to be served concurrently, and $13,250 in fines. With good behavior, she will be out in considerably less time. At the time of this writing, the female hired to replace her in the tailor shop was suspended and is under investigation for similar behavior. Where was the deterrent for engaging in this behavior? After all, Joyce Mitchell, Gene Palmer, and Denise Prell were all given sweetheart deals.

Many others involved in the misconduct were allowed to resign. It was common knowledge that one female employee who was very involved with Gene desperately tried to destroy in excess of eighty unauthorized inmate personal TV permits with smiley faces on them – a code used by Gene to easily identify the fake permits.

Although never charged, she and others are no longer employed by New York State. No longer employed, but not charged with any criminal activity either. What message does this send?

The message received was that it told many of us that Governor Cuomo wanted this wrapped up, sealed, and the truth never to be made known to the public. It will remain suppressed, protected by confidentiality acknowledgments and conditions of retirement. It will be hidden from view, kept underground in the tunnels, and obscured by the cold, gray physical wall of the facility, forever.

Afterword

Countless people throughout my career commented that books about the Clinton Correctional Facility were waiting to be written. Each employee there had a story that they wanted to be told.

Clinton was never the mess that the media portrayed it to be. It was simply a hard place for hard convicts. If someone had a tough case that they couldn't handle, they usually ended up with us.

My story has now been told. This book is for all of the good, honest men and women who wore the blue or gray uniform pants with pride; the civilian staff who helped keep the facility running smoothly, without acknowledgment or being told "Good job!"; for all of the employees who took pride in their job and made a difference in their communities; for those who suffer from Post-Traumatic Stress Disorder and those who are the voice for them; for those of us still living after those we worked with committed suicide or heinous acts, leaving us with questions as to why.

I appreciate that my employment for over 26 years allowed me to develop, promote, and sell my skills. It allowed me to provide well for my family, live comfortably and put my son through a private engineering university. It allowed me the ability to travel throughout the USA and enjoy the company of corporate executives before my performances when just 24 hours earlier I was supervising a roach-infested observation area with a stench permeating the air.

The public could never understand what most of us have endured. They believed that we sat at desks while the inmates were locked up in their cells. They never knew of the violence, the stress, and the hate toward us. They would know even less of the additional stressors from those not only above but amongst us as well. All of these factors resulted in us being rewarded with a much shorter life expectancy than other occupations.

Some will forever be a prisoner within the steel and concrete of the facility, but those who worked there have a part of us that remains in Clinton, the part of us unable to escape the invisible walls of Dannemora.

Last Badge issued to the Author before his Retirement

"Lord, Be Merciful To Me, a Fool!"

— An excerpt of "The Fool's Prayer"
by Edward Rowland Sill (1841-1887)